Targeting PHONICS

★ Book 1 ★

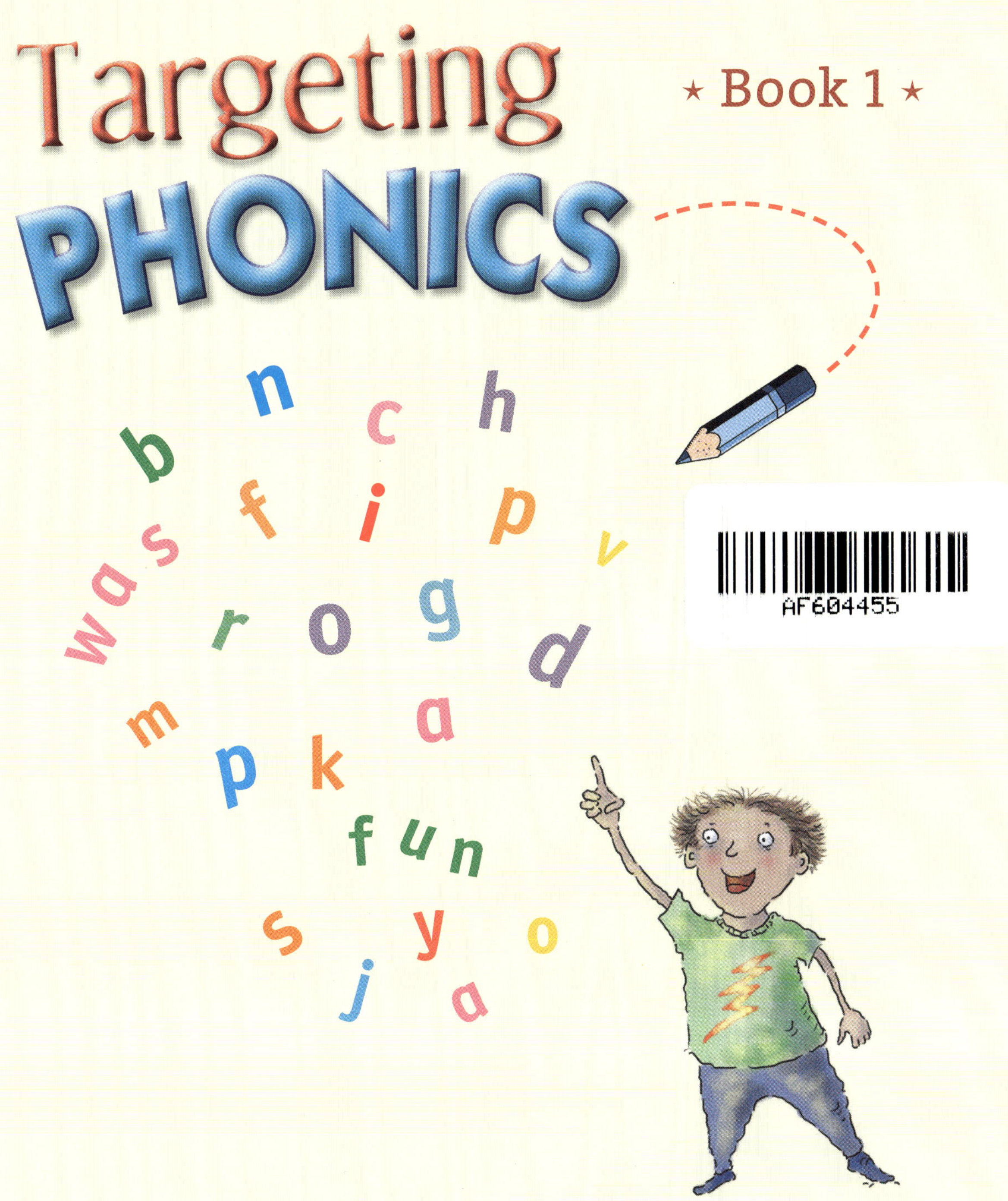

This book belongs to

....

....

Targeting Phonics Book 1

Reprinted 2023, 2024

ISBN: 978-1-92572-634-3

Published by Pascal Press
PO Box 250
Glebe NSW 2037
www.pascalpress.com.au
contact@pascalpress.com.au

Author: Norah Colvin
Publisher: Lynn Dickinson
Designer: Janice Bowles
Illustrations by Paul Lennon & Janice Bowles
Typesetting: BSMART Publishing
Printed by Vivar Printing/Green Giant Press

★ Contents ★

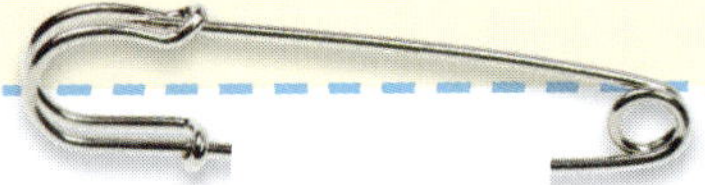

⋆ Phonics explained ⋆

Phonics helps children decode words for reading
and encode words for spelling.

Decoding requires them to see the letters, match them with a sound and blend the sounds together to say the word.
Encoding requires them to hear the sounds in a word and match each sound with a corresponding letter or combination of letters.
The ability to decode and encode words efficiently underpins success with reading and writing.

The ***Targeting Phonics*** series uses a systematic ***synthetic phonics*** approach with reference to the progression recommended in the Australian Curriculum. It introduces students to the 26 letters of the alphabet (*graphemes*) and their relationship to the 44 sounds (*phonemes*) of the English language, which the letters represent.

The ***synthetic phonics*** approach encourages children to listen to all the phonemes (individual sounds) and blend or 'synthesise' them to form words, such as 'b' + 'a' + 't' = bat. Reading and spelling are taught in relationship to each other — if you can read a word, you can spell it. Writing the words also helps to consolidate this learning and is included in every unit.

Prior to the synthetic phonics methodology, schools often used ***analytic phonics***, where children were encouraged to identify the sound of the first letter and guess the rest of the word using rhymes or word-building strategies such as onset and rime. Reading and spelling were taught as separate skills, rather than being integrated.

⋆ About the author ⋆

Norah Colvin is a teacher with over 20 years' experience in early childhood classrooms. She is passionate about literacy education and enjoys sharing children's first steps into literacy. She has also supported learners who experienced difficulty attaining literacy skills the first time round.

⋆ How to use this book ⋆

Students are introduced to each of the 26 letters of the alphabet and their most common sounds. This includes the 21 **consonants** introduced initially at the beginning of words and the five short **vowels**.

The introduction of the letters follows this sequence:

s, a, t, p, n, i, d, m, g, o, c, b, h, e, r, u, f, l, j, k, v, w, y, z, q, x

Each letter page starts with photographic sound cards of four things that begin with the letter and sound. These sound cards can be accessed online using the QR code on the page for an image and audio pronunciation of the sound. Students should watch and listen to the sound card for each letter before completing the activity.

Each unit provides activities for students to blend sounds to make and spell words using **graphemes**.

Activities are reviewed at the end of each unit of four new letters, with a full review included at the end of the book.

Read and Spell

When students have learned sufficient letters and sounds, they read **decodable** words by blending known graphemes to form:

CV, VC, CVC, CCVC, CVCC words. *Note: C= consonant, V= vowel*

Students read sentences formed from a combination of those decodable words and a small number of sight words introduced in each unit starting from Unit 2.

Students spell decodable words by stretching out the sounds in CV, VC, CVC, CCVC, CVCC words formed from known graphemes. Lists of decodable words are included in the back of the book.

High Frequency Words

Students learn to recognise by sight a number of high frequency words in each unit starting from Unit 2. Lists of high frequency words are included in the back of the book.

Comprehension

Students read sentences and short paragraphs formed using decodable and known high-frequency words to practise reading and comprehension skills.

It is suggested that students proceed through the book, completing the lessons in sequence, to ensure that all words encountered in activities have already been learned, either as decodable words or high frequency words.

★ Glossary ★

Analytic phonics	starts with a word and takes it apart to identify its parts, *for example: 'bat' = 'b' + 'at'*
Consonants	are produced when the air is restricted in some way; in English there are 24 consonant sounds, most of which are represented by one letter and some which are represented by two letters, such as 'sh' and 'ch'
Decode	see the letters, match them with a sound and blend the sounds together to say the word
Digraph	a combination of two letters representing one sound, *for example: 'sh' as in 'shoe', 'ch' as in 'church', 'th' as in 'thimble' or 'there', 'oa' as in 'boat' or 'ea' as in 'peach'*
Encode	listen to the sounds in a word and write the corresponding letter or combination of letters to match each sound
Graphemes	letters used to represent the sounds of the language
Phonemes	individual units of sound heard in the language
Phonics	the relationships between graphemes and phonemes; understanding how letters and groups of letters are used to represent the sounds of the language
Phonemic awareness	the ability to hear and manipulate different sounds in words
Split digraph	when the two letters that represent one sound are split by another letter, *for example: ae as in 'cake'*
Synthetic phonics	starts with individual sounds and blends them together to form words, *for example: 'b' + 'a' + 't' = 'bat'*
Trigraphs	three letters used to represent one sound, *for example: 'igh' as in 'high' or 'light'*
Quadgraphs	four letters used to represent one sound, *for example: 'eigh' as in 'eight' or 'weight'*
Vowels	sounds formed without obstruction to the flow of air by the tongue, teeth or lips; usually represented by the letters 'a', 'e', 'i', 'o', and 'u', either individually or in combination; the letters are sometimes combined with 'y' as in 'boy' or 'w' as in 'cow'; a vowel is usually necessary in every word and syllable in the English language

★ Version 9.0 Australian Curriculum correlations ★

Targeting Phonics Book 1 teaches students to recognise and name all upper- and lower-case letters (graphs) and know the most common sound that each letter represents. (AC9EFLY11)
This includes the 21 single-letter consonants and 5 short vowel sounds. In addition, students will:

- Write consonant–vowel–consonant (CVC) words by representing sounds with the appropriate letters, and blend sounds associated with letters when reading CVC words (AC9EFLY12)
- Use knowledge of letters and sounds to spell words (AC9EFLY13)
- Read and write some high frequency words and other familiar words (AC9EFLY14)
- Use comprehension strategies such as visualising, predicting, connecting, summarising and questioning to understand and discuss texts listened to, viewed or read independently (AC9EFLY05)
- Read decodable and authentic texts using developing phonic knowledge, and monitor meaning using context and emerging grammatical knowledge (AC9EFLY04)
- Form most lower-case and upper-case letters using learnt letter formations (AC9EFLY08)

  ISBN: 9781925726343

★ Games to teach decoding & encoding skills ★

Games provide students with fun opportunities to practise their decoding skills and to reinforce their recognition of high-frequency words.

★ Let's make a word ★

You need: Letter tiles, at least one of each letter of the alphabet and 4 of each of the vowels: a, e, i, o, and u. Use purchased or Scrabble tiles or make your own by writing the letters in small squares on paper or card and then laminating before cutting out.

The game can be played with one or more children with or without an adult.

How to play:

1. Place the tiles face down on the table.
2. Players take turns to take one tile and place it face up in front of them. They continue taking tiles, one at a time, until a word can be made.
   The word must be blended and read.
3. As a word is made, it is placed to the side and the game continues until all the tiles have been used and all possible words have been made from the tiles.
   The player with the most complete words wins.

★ Games to teach high frequency words ★

★ Your choice bingo ★

You need: Word cards from the back of this book. Photocopy then laminate and cut out. A pencil, a highlighter and a sheet of A4 paper for each child. Players fold their paper in half along the long edge, then fold it in half again. They then fold it in half again from end to end. Open it out and they have divided their page into eight boxes.

How to play:

1. Place the words face up on the table. Children choose eight words and write them onto their bingo sheet, one in each box.
2. Turn over and shuffle the word cards.
3. As you call each word, players highlight the box if the word is written on their sheet. The first to complete their sheet is the winner.

★ Bucket ★

You need: Word cards from the back of the book, photocopied, cut and laminated. Four similar cards with the word bucket written on them.

How to play:

1. Place all the word cards, including bucket cards, into a small bucket.
2. Children take turns to take a word from the bucket. If they can read the word they keep it. Then it is the next child's turn. If they take the word bucket, they must place all their words back into the bucket. The word bucket is then put aside.
3. The winner is the child with the most words when no words remain in the bucket. Because the game involves a certain amount of luck as well as recognising words, everyone has a chance of winning.

  ISBN: 9781925726343

Aa Bb Cc Dd Ee Ff Gg Hh Ii Jj Kk Ll Mm Nn Oo Pp Qq Rr **Ss** Tt Uu Vv Ww Xx Yy Zz

Consonant sound s as in *snake*

S s

Use this QR code to watch and listen to the letter S sound cards below

 snake	 sun
 star	 slug

Space hound Sam loves to walk on stars. His favourites have the letter **Ss** on them. Colour them yellow for him.

  ISBN: 9781925726343

Consonant sound s as in *snake*

Say the names of the pictures below.
Colour the pictures that begin with the letter 's'.

Handwriting

Track these letters

Trace these letters

 ISBN: 9781925726343

Short vowel sound  as in *ant*

Use this QR code to watch and listen to the **letter A** sound cards below

Only the apples with the letter **A** and **a** are red, the rest are green. Colour them all the correct colour.

  ISBN: 9781925726343

Short vowel sound a as in *ant*

Say the names of the pictures below.
Colour the pictures that begin with the letter 'a'.

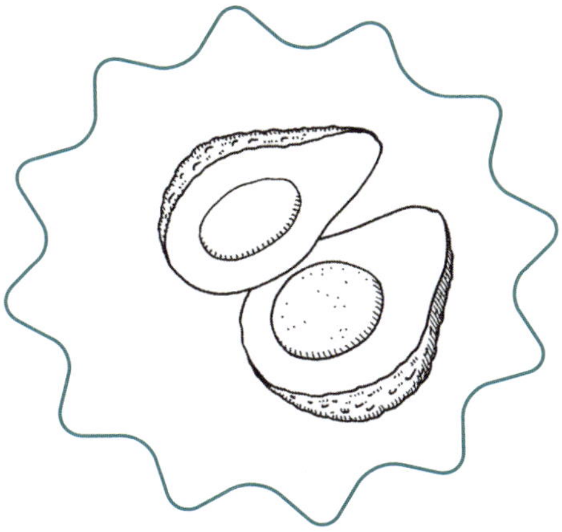

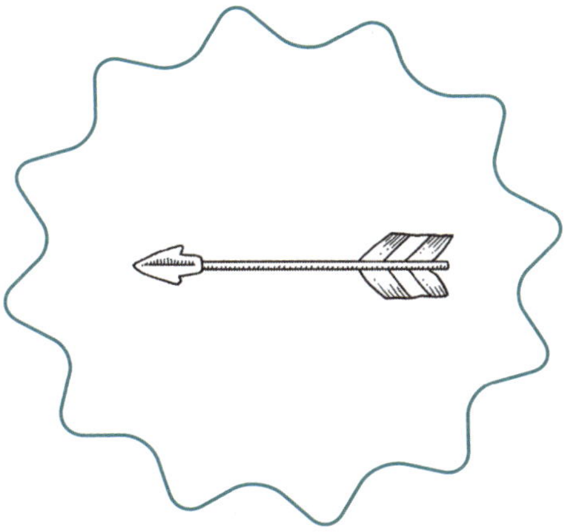

Handwriting

Track these letters

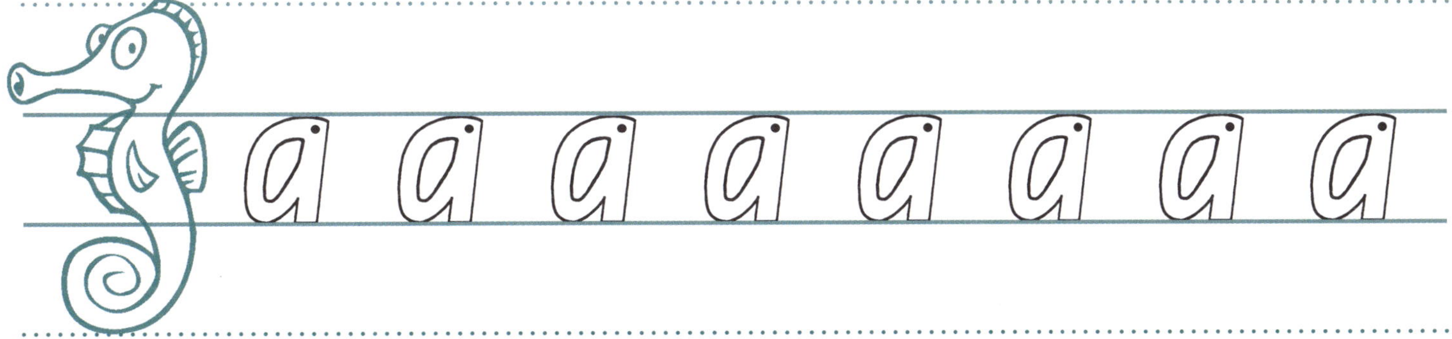

Trace these letters

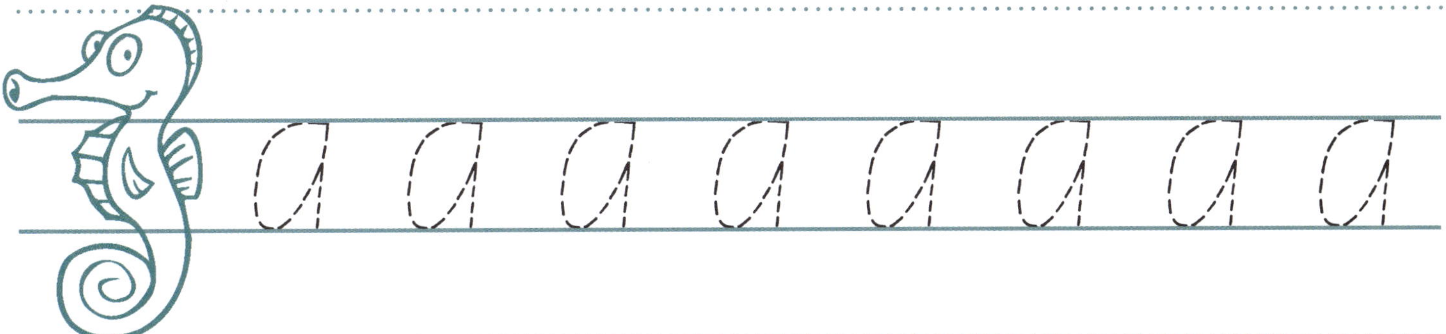

  ISBN: 9781925726343

Aa Bb Cc Dd Ee Ff Gg Hh Ii Jj Kk Ll Mm Nn Oo Pp Qq Rr Ss **Tt** Uu Vv Ww Xx Yy Zz

Consonant sound  t as in *turtle*

T t

Use this QR code to watch and listen to the **letter T** sound cards below

 turtle	 table
 tiger	  taxi

Trudy Trickster loves the letter **Tt**. How many can you see?'

  ISBN: 9781925726343

Consonant sound t as in *turtle*

Say the names of the pictures below.
Colour pictures that begin with the letter 't'.

Handwriting

Track these letters

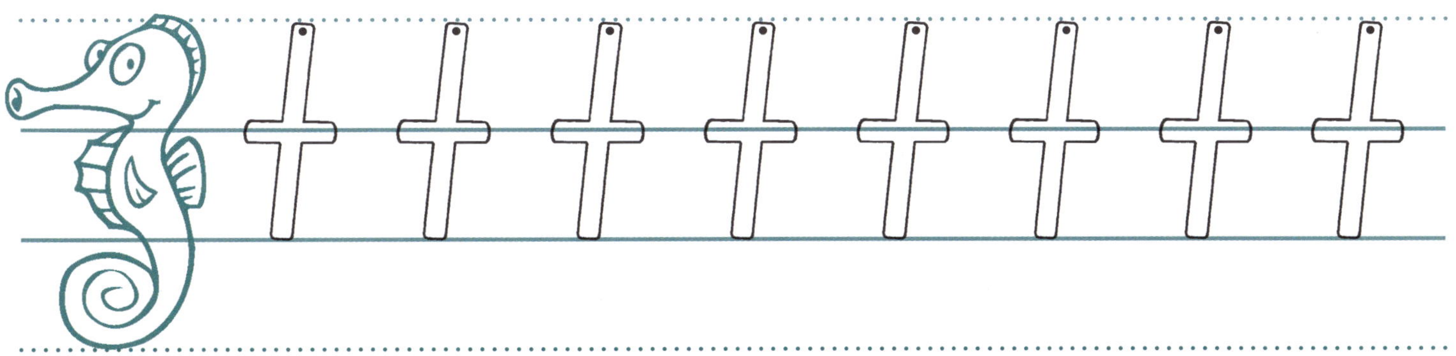

Trace these letters

  ISBN: 9781925726343

Aa Bb Cc Dd Ee Ff Gg Hh Ii Jj Kk Ll Mm Nn Oo Pp Qq Rr Ss Tt Uu Vv Ww Xx Yy Zz

Consonant sound  p as in *puppy*

P p

Use this QR code to watch and listen to the **letter P** sound cards below

 puppy	 panda
 pizza	 pancakes

a k n r p P c t p p p s p p H v b P p P W x

Help Patsy Possum find her favourite flowers by colouring the **Pp** path.

  ISBN: 9781925726343

Consonant sound p as in *puppy*

Say the names of the pictures below.
Colour pictures that begin with the letter 'p'.

Handwriting

Track these letters

Trace these letters

Aa Bb Cc Dd Ee Ff Gg Hh Ii Jj Kk Ll Mm Nn Oo Pp Qq Rr Ss Tt Uu Vv Ww Xx Yy Zz

⋆ Review ⋆

Say the names of the pictures below. Draw a circle around the beginning sound.

Say the names of the pictures below. Write the beginning sound.

Say the names of the pictures below. Draw a circle around the end sound of each word.

  ISBN: 9781925726343

Decoding

Now you know these letters and sounds: s a t p

Blend them to make and read the words: at, sat, pat, pats, app, tap

Say the sounds	Blend the sounds	Read the word
Point to each letter as you say the sound.	Slide your finger from one sound to the next as you say the sound.	Point to the word as you read it.
a t	a‿t	at
s a t	s‿a‿t	sat
p a t	p‿a‿t	pat
p a t s	p‿a‿t‿s	pats
a p p	a‿p‿p	app
t a p	t‿a‿p	tap

Spelling

Now you can read these words, you can write them too.

Trace the words. Then write them on the lines below.

at sat pat

pats tap taps

Choose one of the letters you know to complete these words.
Read the words.

s__t __at ta__ pat__ __at __pp

  ISBN: 9781925726343

Aa Bb Cc Dd Ee Ff Gg Hh Ii Jj Kk Ll Mm **Nn** Oo Pp Qq Rr Ss Tt Uu Vv Ww Xx Yy Zz

Consonant sound  as in *numbat*

N n

Use this QR code to watch and listen to the **letter N** sound cards below

 numbat	 nut
 nest	 ninja

Narine wants a letter **Nn** for each of her pups. Are there enough? Circle them.

Consonant sound n as in *numbat*

Say the names of the pictures below.
Colour the pictures that begin with the letter 'n'.

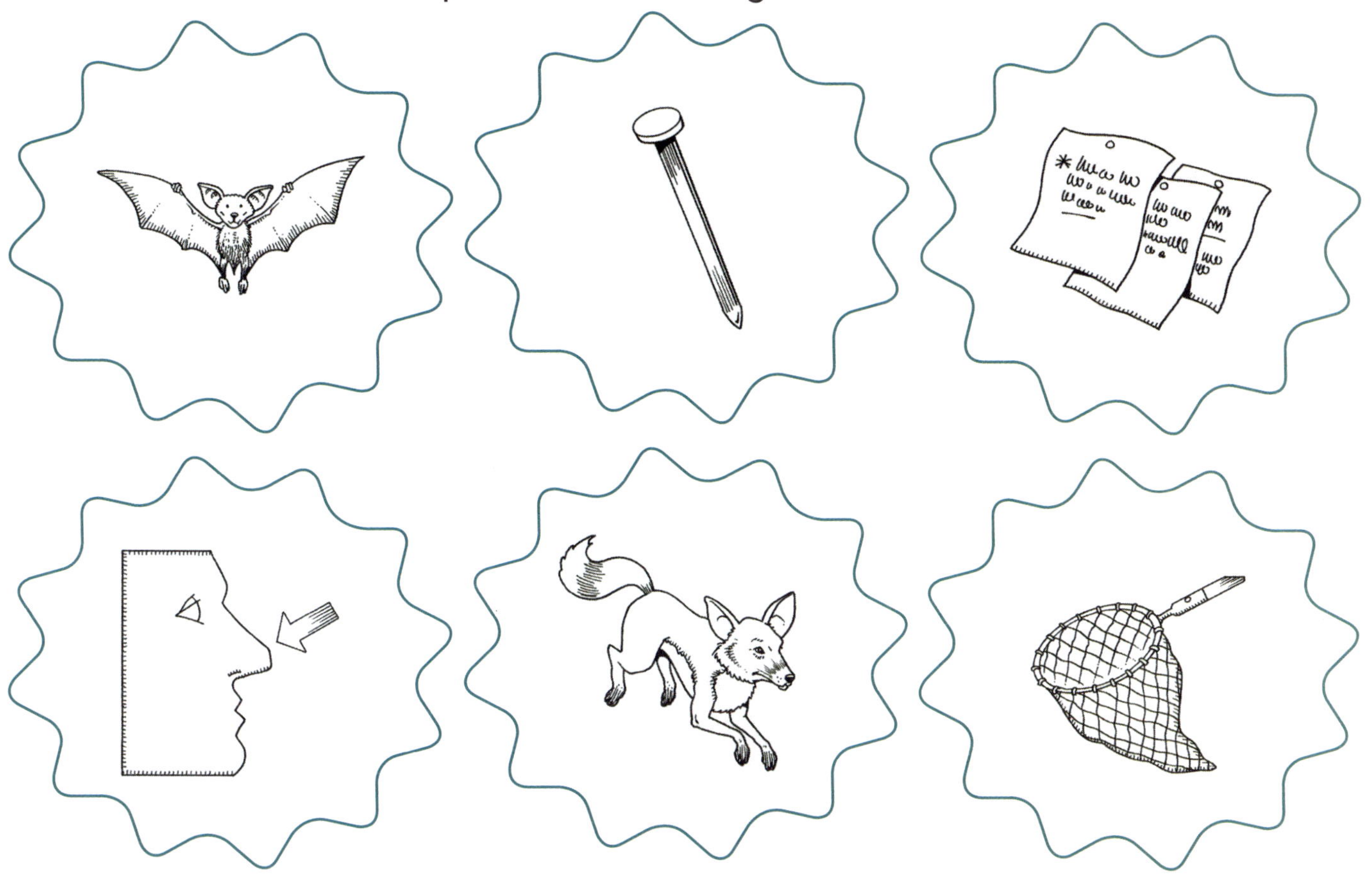

Handwriting

Track these letters

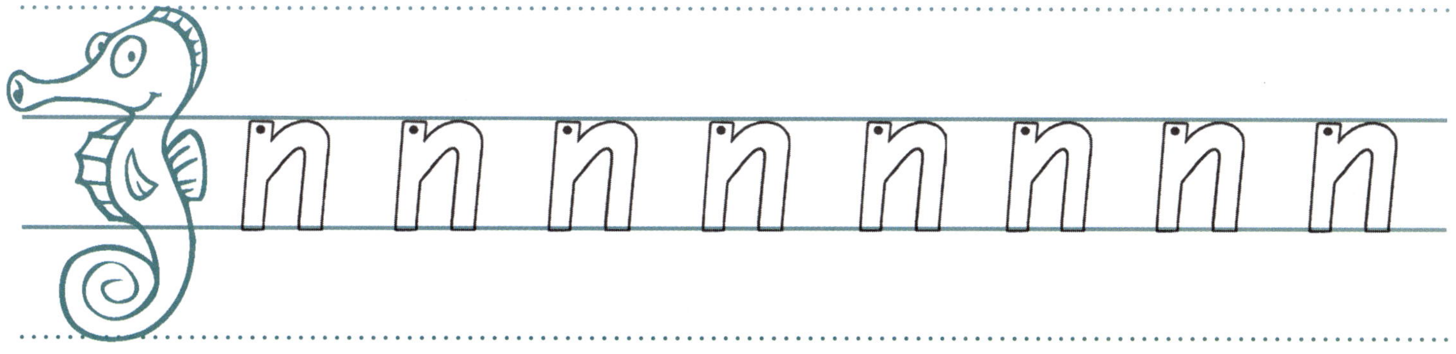

Trace these letters

  ISBN: 9781925726343

Aa Bb Cc Dd Ee Ff Gg Hh **Ii** Jj Kk Ll Mm Nn Oo pp Qq Rr Ss Tt Uu Vv Ww Xx Yy Zz

Short vowel sound  as in *insect*

Use this QR code to watch and listen to the **letter I** sound cards below

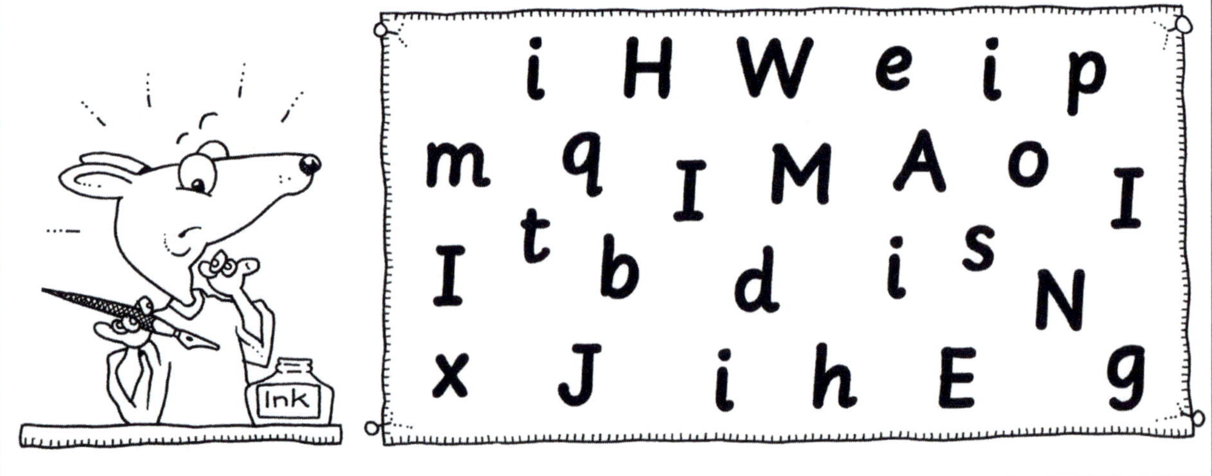

Inky Mouse needs to circle the letter **Ii**s on his paper. Can you help him?

  ISBN: 9781925726343

Short vowel sound i as in *insect*

Say the names of the pictures below.
Colour pictures that begin with the letter 'i'.

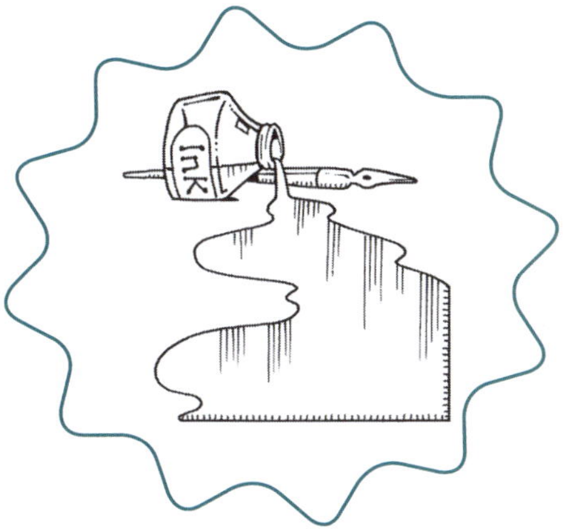

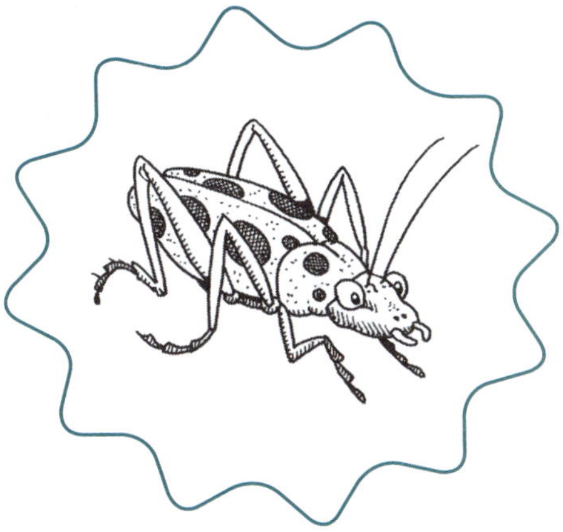

Handwriting

Track these letters

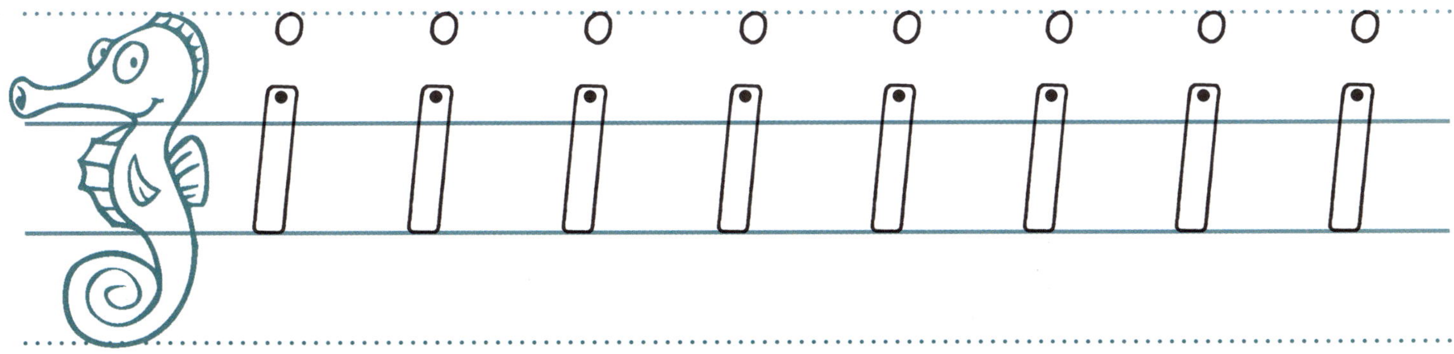

Trace these letters

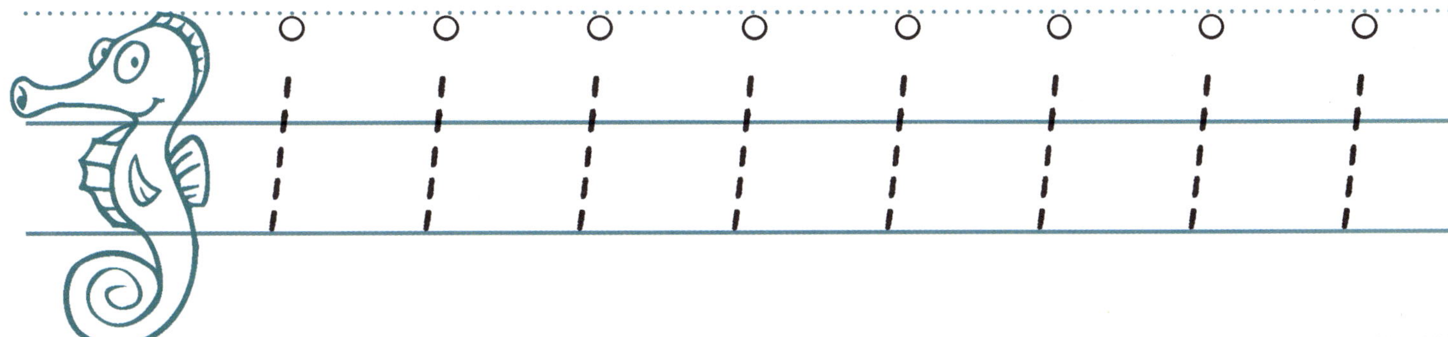

  ISBN: 9781925726343

Aa Bb Cc **Dd** Ee Ff Gg Hh Ii Jj Kk Ll Mm Nn Oo Pp Qq Rr Ss Tt Uu Vv Ww Xx Yy Zz

Consonant sound  as in *dog*

Use this QR code to watch and listen to the **letter D** sound cards below

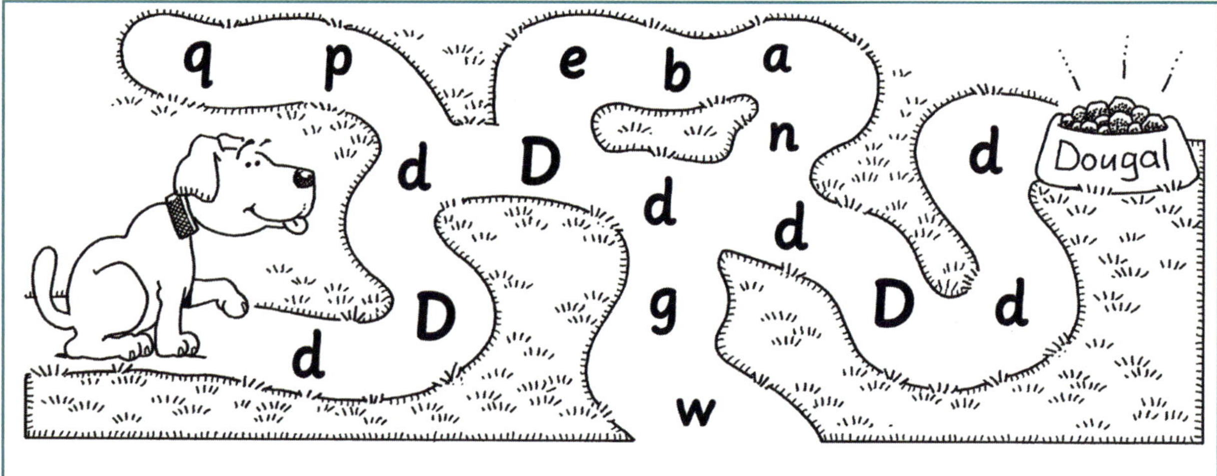

Follow the **Dd**s for Dougal's food.

Consonant sound **d** as in *dog*

Say the names of the pictures below.
Colour pictures that begin with the letter 'd'.

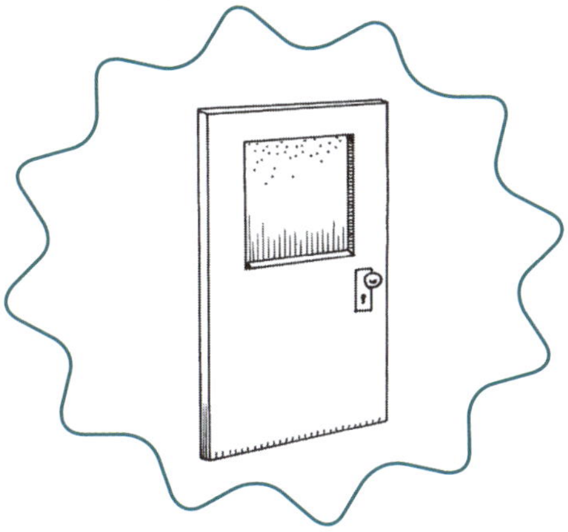

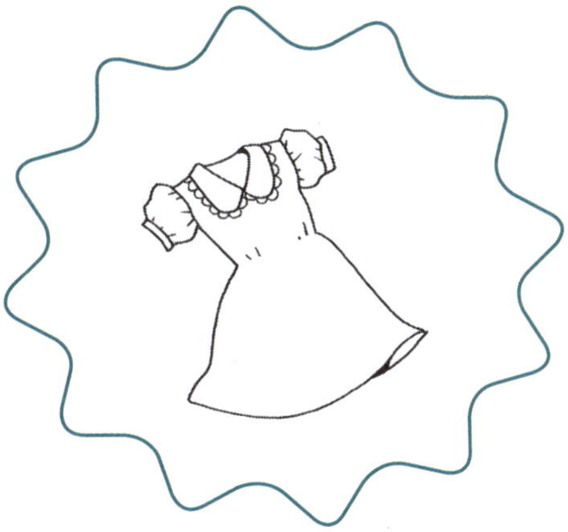

Handwriting

Track these letters

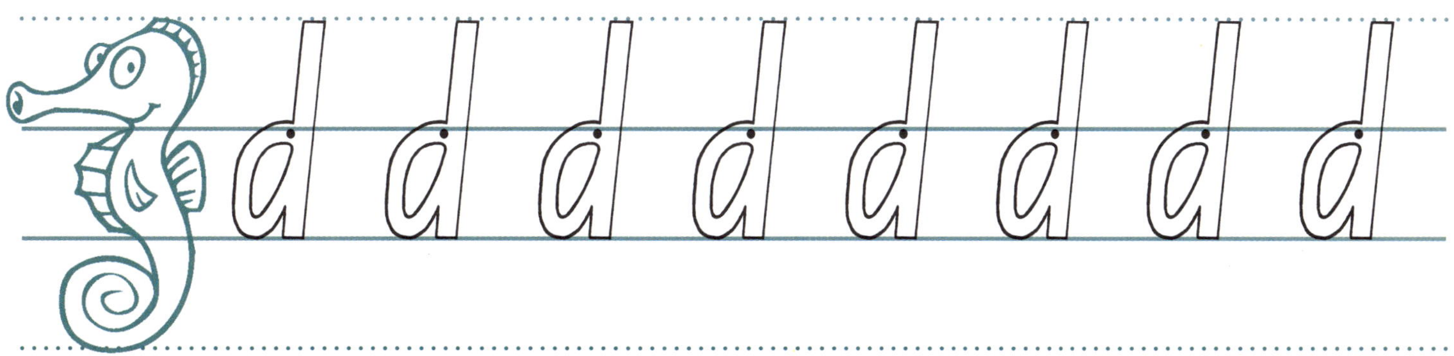

Trace these letters

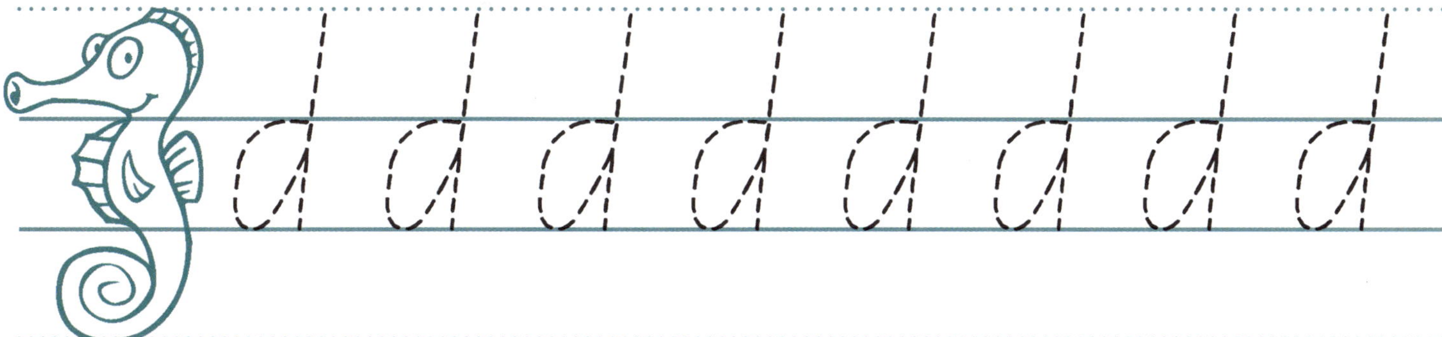

  ISBN: 9781925726343

Aa Bb Cc Dd Ee Ff Gg Hh Ii Jj Kk Ll **Mm** Nn Oo Pp Qq Rr Ss Tt Uu Vv Ww Xx Yy Zz

Consonant sound m as in *mouse*

Use this QR code to watch and listen to the **letter M** sound cards below

Mandy is heading for the Moon. Colour the **Mm** stars for her to find her way.

 © PASCAL PRESS ISBN: 9781925726343

Consonant sound m as in *mouse*

Say the names of the pictures below.
Colour pictures that begin with the letter 'm'.

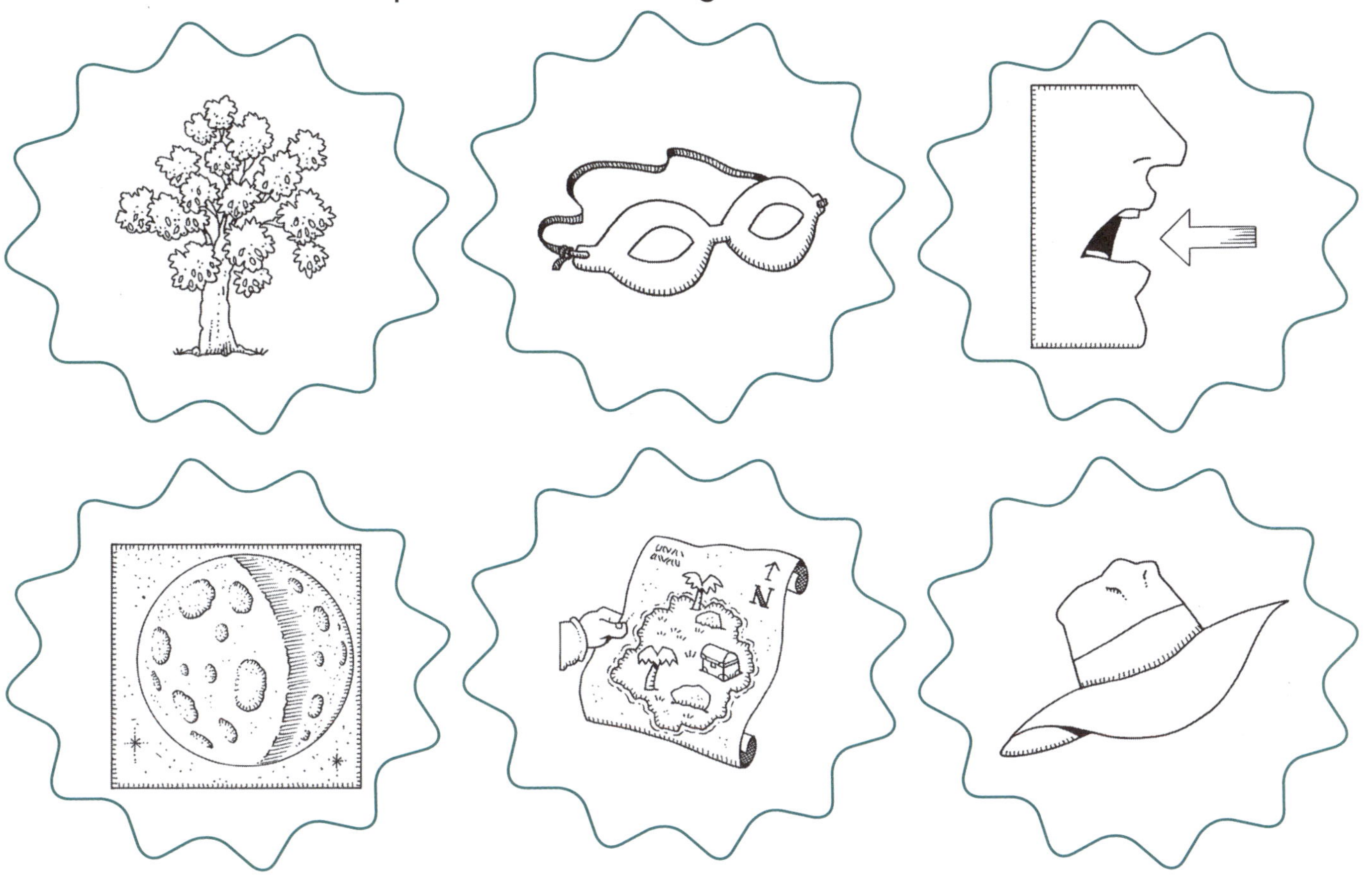

Handwriting

Track these letters

Trace these letters

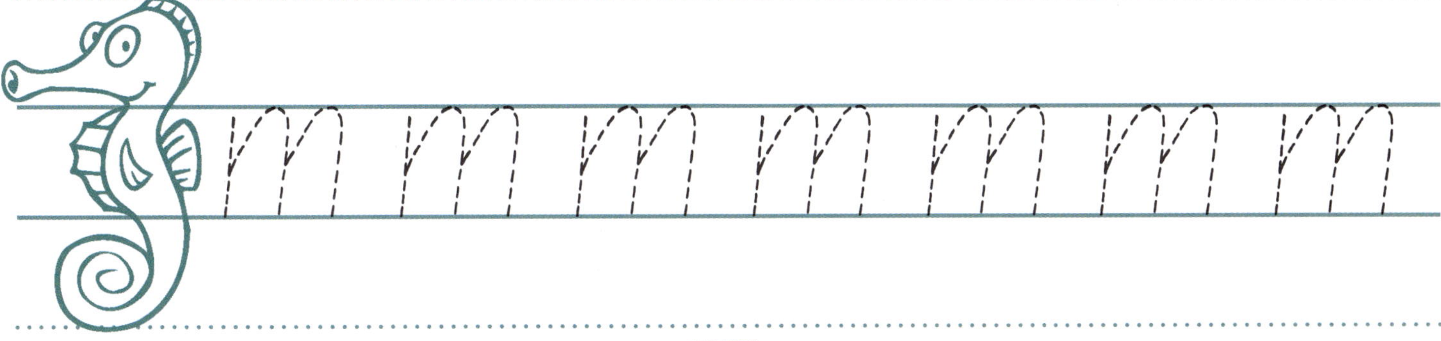

  ISBN: 9781925726343

Aa Bb Cc Dd Ee Ff Gg Hh Ii Jj Kk Ll Mm Nn Oo Pp Qq Rr Ss Tt Uu Vv Ww Xx Yy Zz

⋆ Review ⋆

Say the names of the pictures below. Draw a circle around the beginning sound.

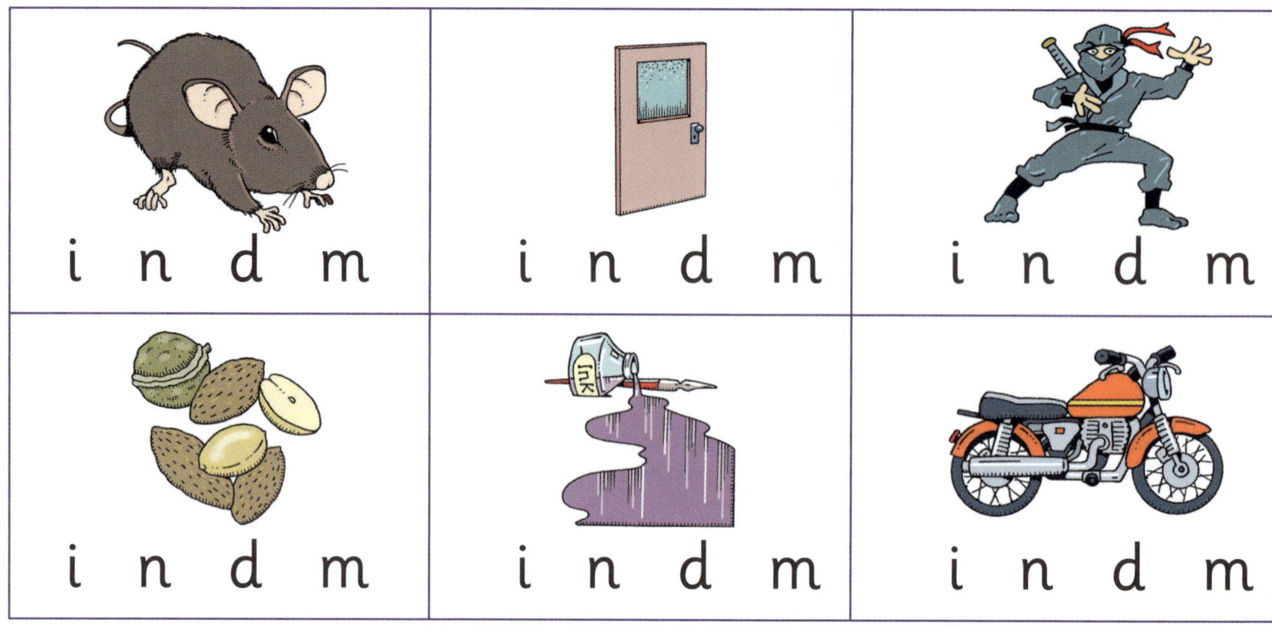

Say the names of the pictures below. Write the beginning sound.

Say the names of the pictures below. Draw a circle around the end sound.

  ISBN: 9781925726343

Decoding

Now you know these letters and sounds: i n d m and s a t p

You can blend them to make and read the words: in, pad, it, nit, am, dam, an, and, sip, pip

Say the sounds	Blend the sounds	Read the word
Point to each letter as you say the sound.	Slide your finger from one sound to the next as you say the sound.	Point to the word as you read it.
i n	i‿n	in
p a d	p‿a‿d	pad
i t	i‿t	it
n i t	n‿i‿t	nit
a m	a‿m	am
d a m	d‿a‿m	dam
a n	a‿n	an
a n d	a‿n‿d	and
s i p	s‿i‿p	sip
p i p	p‿i‿p	pip

Read the words. Draw lines to match them to the pictures.

  ISBN: 9781925726343

Spelling

Now you can read these words, you can write them too.
Trace the words. Then write them on the lines below.

din sap pat

pit Sam Dan

sand dim Tim

dip tip mint

Choose one of the letters you know to complete these words.
Read the words.

s__p __at ti__

p__n ma__ __in

High frequency words – Set 1

Learn these words.

I	a	the	this	is
see	A	The	This	on

Comprehension

Read the sentences. Draw a picture to match.

I sit on a mat.	Dan is a man.

This is a tap.	I see the map.

  ISBN: 9781925726343

Aa Bb Cc Dd Ee Ff Gg Hh Ii Jj Kk Ll Mm Nn Oo Pp Qq Rr Ss Tt Uu Vv Ww Xx Yy Zz

Consonant sound  as in *goat*

G g

Use this QR code to watch and listen to the **letter G** sound cards below

goat

ghost

grass

gloves

Find Gogo Goose's lost **Gg** eggs and colour them gold.

  ISBN: 9781925726343

Consonant sound g as in *goat*

Say the names of the pictures below.
Colour pictures that begin with the letter 'g'.

Handwriting

Track these letters

Trace these letters

Aa Bb Cc Dd Ee Ff Gg Hh Ii Jj Kk Ll Mm Nn **Oo** Pp Qq Rr Ss Tt Uu Vv Ww Xx Yy Zz

Short vowel sound  as in *octopus*

Use this QR code to watch and listen to the **letter O** sound cards below

 octopus	 orange
 otter	 officer

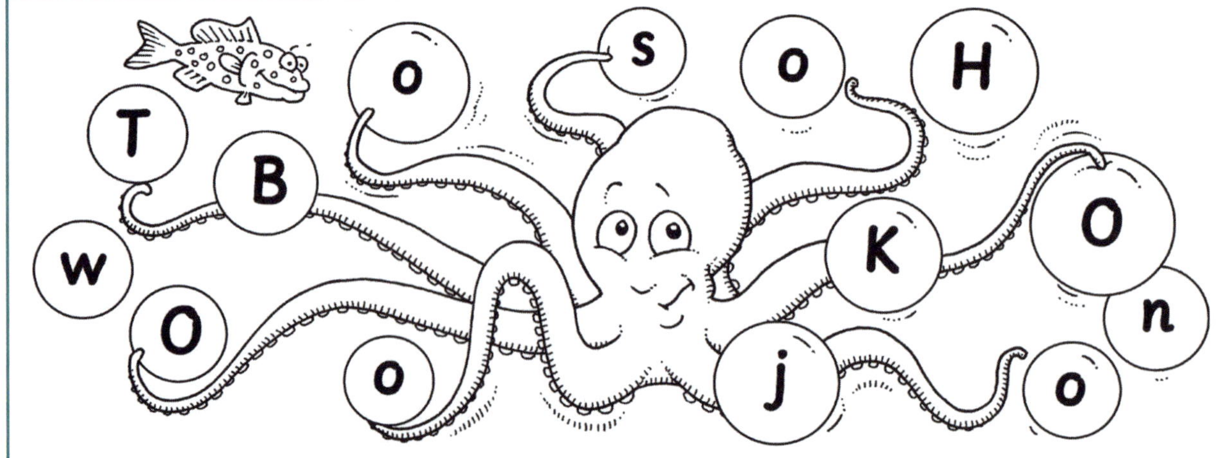

Oscar Octopus collects **Oo** bubbles. Colour them blue for him.

  ISBN: 9781925726343

Short vowel sound o as in *octopus*

Say the names of the pictures below.
Colour pictures that begin with the letter 'o'.

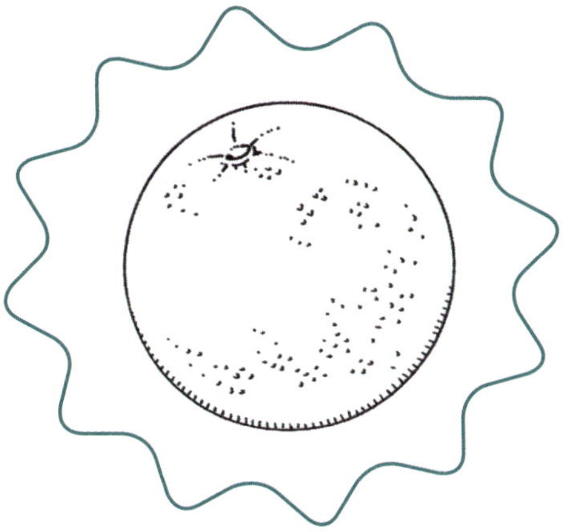

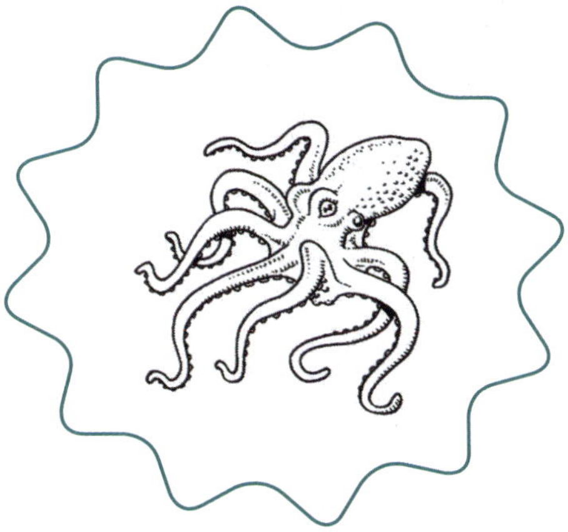

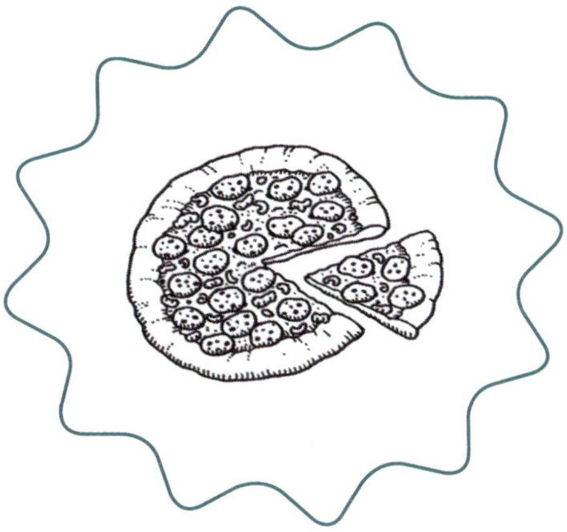

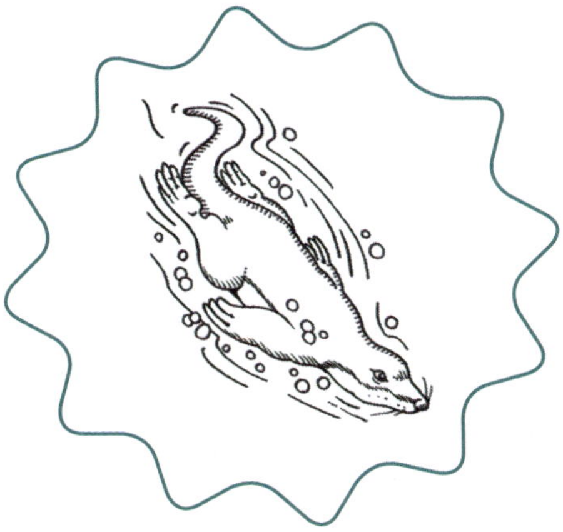

Handwriting

Track these letters

Trace these letters

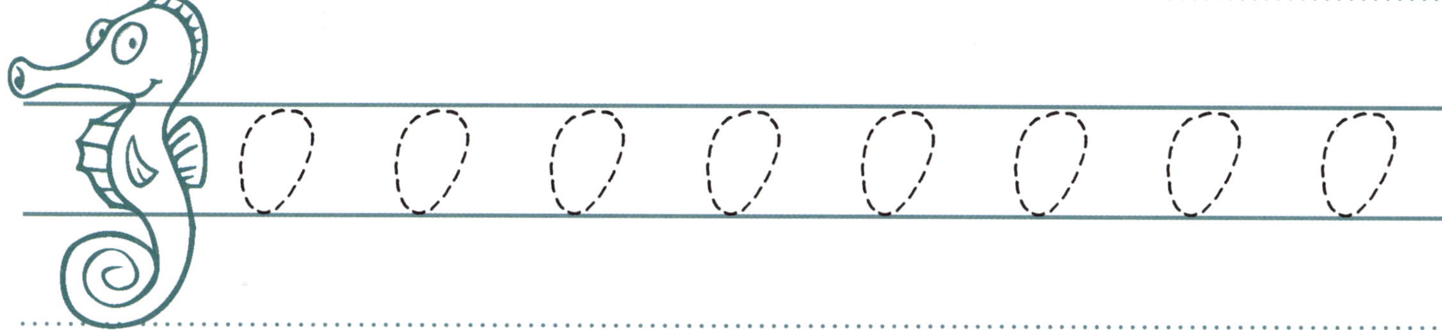

  ISBN: 9781925726343

Aa Bb Cc Dd Ee Ff Gg Hh Ii Jj Kk Ll Mm Nn Oo Pp Qq Rr Ss Tt Uu Vv Ww Xx Yy Zz

Consonant sound  as in *cat*

Use this QR code to watch and listen to the **letter C** sound cards below

Caterpillar loves **Cc** leaves best.
Colour them for her.

Consonant sound c as in *cat*

Say the names of the pictures below.
Colour pictures that begin with the letter 'c'.

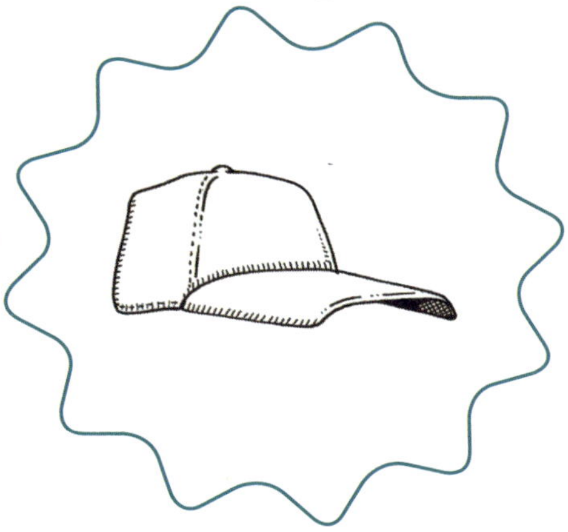

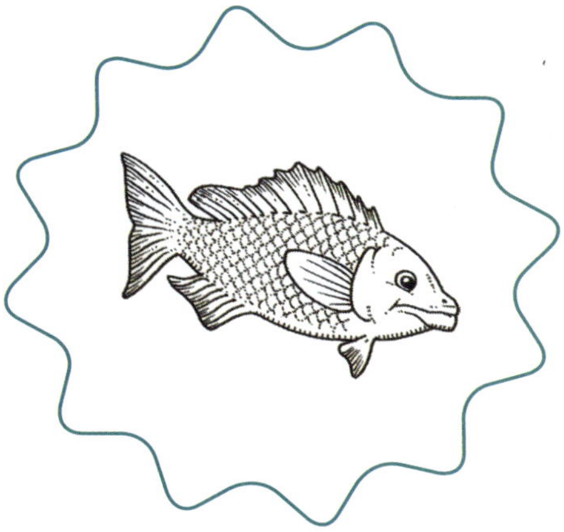

Handwriting

Track these letters

Trace these letters

  ISBN: 9781925726343

Aa
Bb
Cc
Dd
Ee
Ff
Gg
Hh
Ii
Jj
Kk
Ll
Mm
Nn
Oo
Pp
Qq
Rr
Ss
Tt
Uu
Vv
Ww
Xx
Yy
Zz

Consonant sound  as in *bee*

B b

Use this QR code to watch and listen to the **letter B** sound cards below

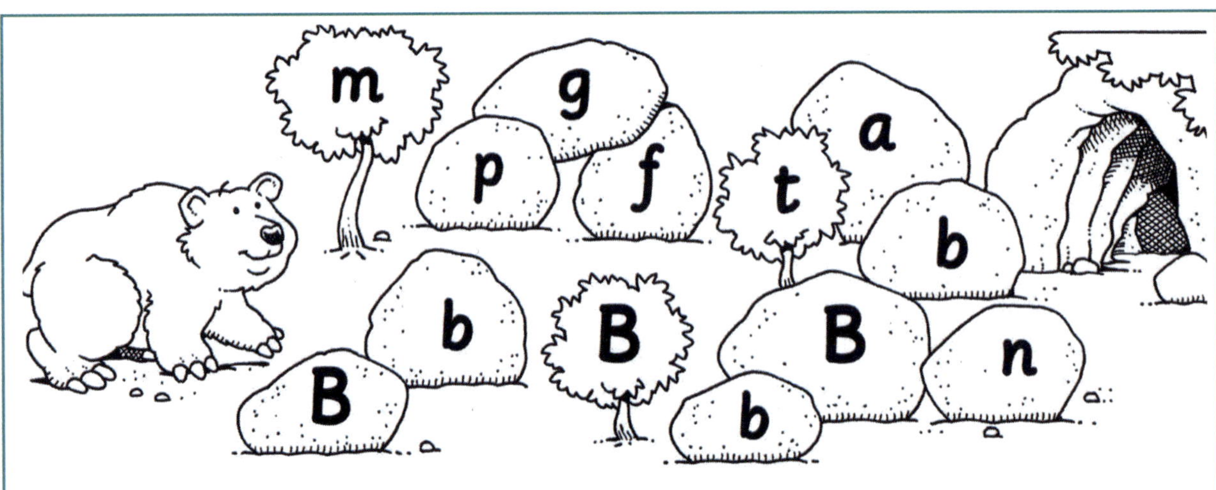

Find Bruno's cave by following the letter **Bb**s.

  ISBN: 9781925726343

Consonant sound b as in *bee*

Say the names of the pictures below.
Colour pictures that begin with the letter 'b'.

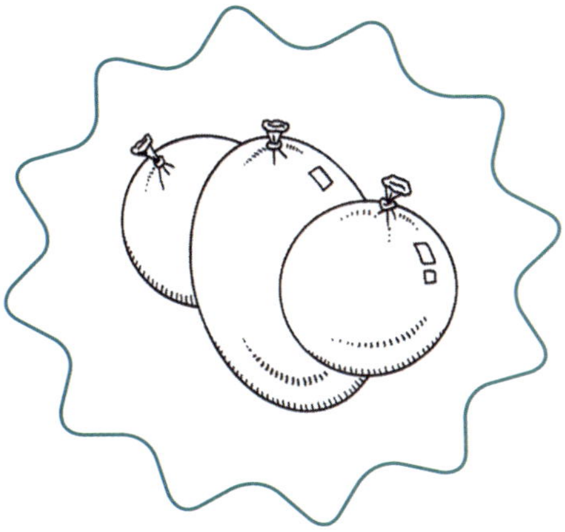

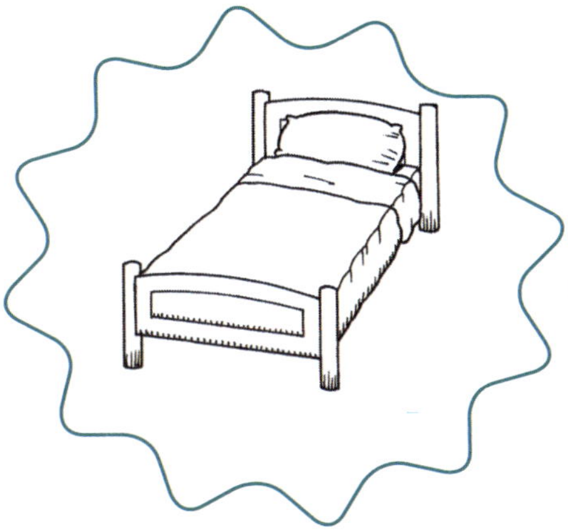

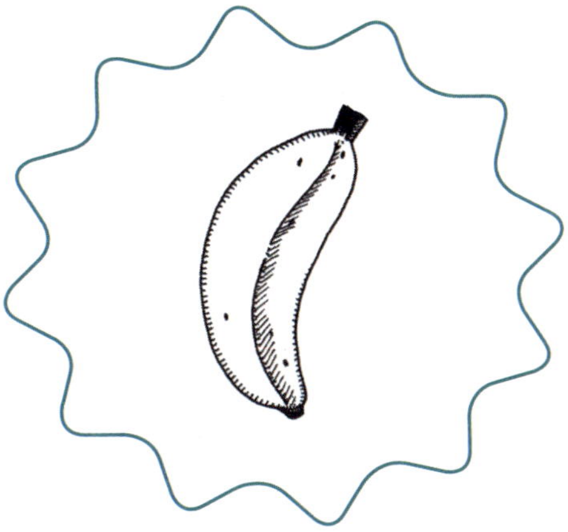

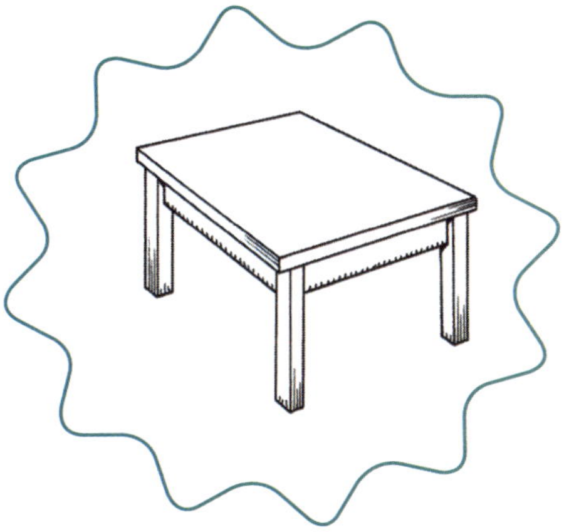

Handwriting

Track these letters

b b b b b b b

Trace these letters

  ISBN: 9781925726343

Aa Bb Cc Dd Ee Ff Gg Hh Ii Jj Kk Ll Mm Nn Oo Pp Qq Rr Ss Tt Uu Vv Ww Xx Yy Zz

⋆ Review ⋆

Name the pictures below. Draw a circle around the sound you hear at the beginning of each word.

g o c b	g o c b	g o c b
g o c b	g o c b	g o c b

Say the names of the pictures below. Write the beginning sound.

Name the pictures below. Draw a circle around the sound you hear at the end of each word.

g c b	g c b	g c b

  ISBN: 9781925726343

Decoding

Now you know these letters and sounds: s a t p i n d m g o c b
You can blend them to make and read the words: cot, bad, sob, dig, cab, tag, gap, bit, act

Say the sounds	Blend the sounds	Read the word
Point to each letter as you say the sound.	Slide your finger from one sound to the next as you say the sound.	Point to the word as you read it.
c o t	c o t	cot
b a d	b a d	bad
s o b	s o b	sob
d i g	d i g	dig
c a b	c a b	cab
t a g	t a g	tag
g a p	g a p	gap
b i t	b i t	bit
a c t	a c t	act

Read the words. Draw lines to match them to the pictures.

cat
bat
bin
pot
mop

dog
cog
pig
bib
bag

  ISBN: 9781925726343

Spelling

Now you can read these words, you can write them too.

Trace the words. Then write them on the lines below.

cap ban dot

togs odd Tom

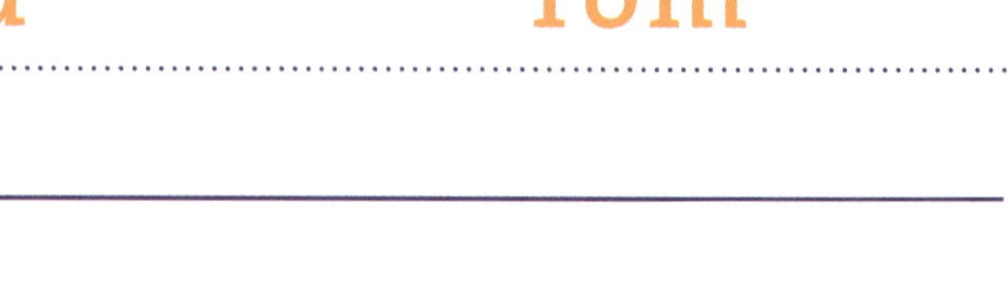

dogs mob big

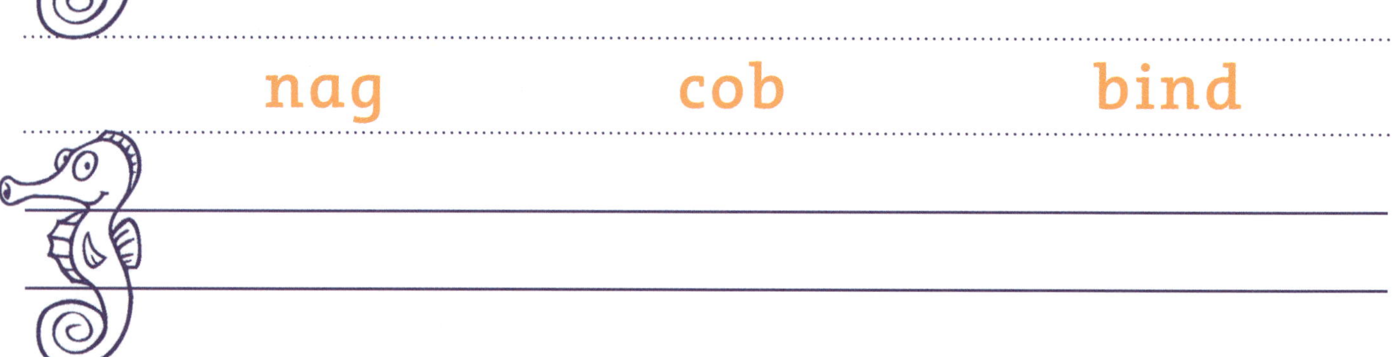

nag cob bind

Choose one of the letters you know to complete these words.
Read the words.

c__p   __ag   bi__

d__g   co__   __ot

  ISBN: 9781925726343

Spelling

Say the names of the pictures below.
Stretch out the word to hear the sound at the beginning, the sound in the middle and the sound at the end.
Write the words on the lines below.

  ISBN: 9781925726343

High frequency words – Set 2

Learn these words.

here	look	that	he	my
Here	Look	That	He	My

Comprehension

Read the sentences. Draw a picture to match.

Here is a big dog. This big dog can dig.	Look at that cat. That cat is bad.

See that man. He is my dad.	This is my top. My top can spin.

  ISBN: 9781925726343

Comprehension

Look at the pictures. Read the sentences. Write in the missing word.

A ___ ___ ___ is in the dam.

The map is in that ___ ___ ___.

This ___ ___ ___ sits on my cap.

This sentence is jumbled. Write it correctly on the lines below.

bat can The see dog the

  ISBN: 9781925726343

Aa Bb Cc Dd Ee Ff Gg **Hh** Ii Jj Kk Ll Mm Nn Oo Pp Qq Rr Ss Tt Uu Vv Ww Xx Yy Zz

Consonant sound  as in *horse*

Use this QR code to watch and listen to the **letter H** sound cards below

 horse	 house
 hat	 hen

Harry likes **Hh** hats best. Colour them so he can find them.

ISBN: 9781925726343

Consonant sound h as in *horse*

Say the names of the pictures below.
Colour pictures that begin with the letter 'h'.

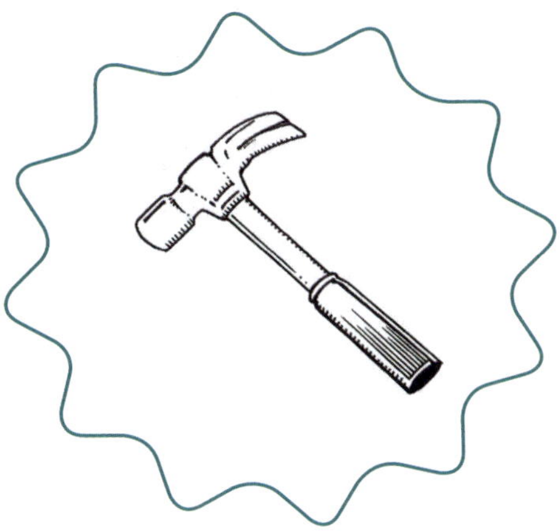

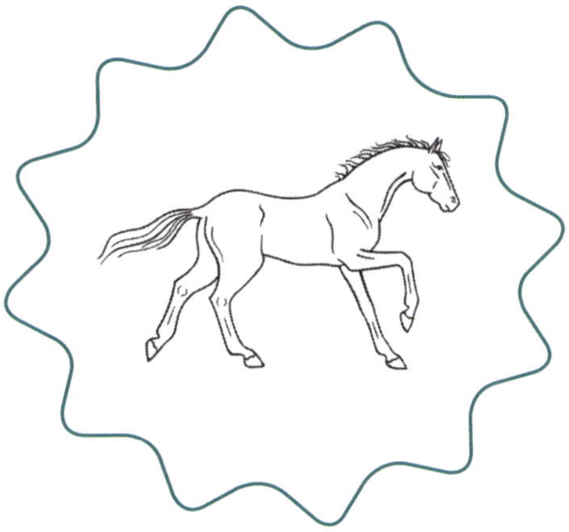

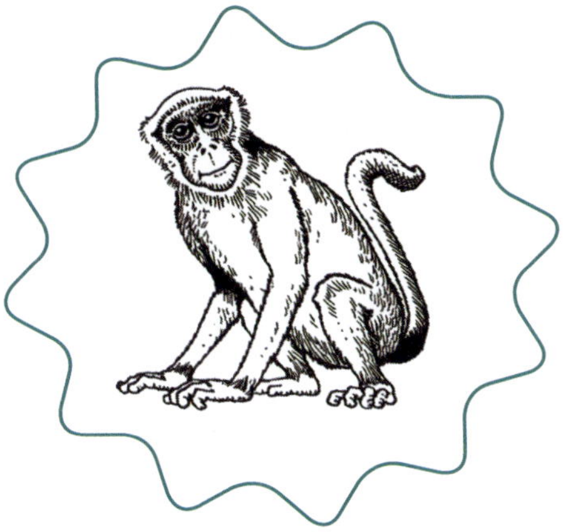

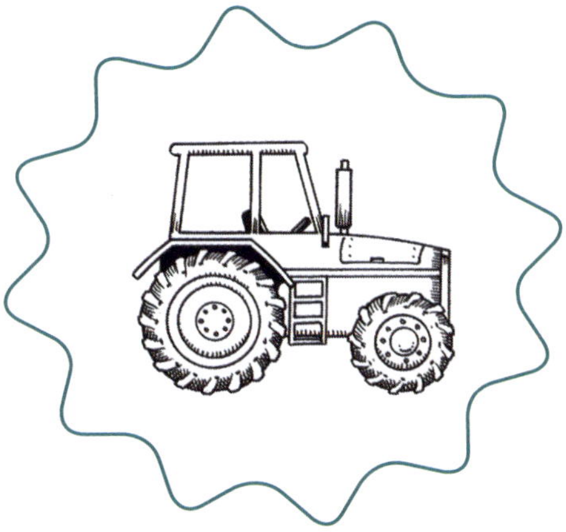

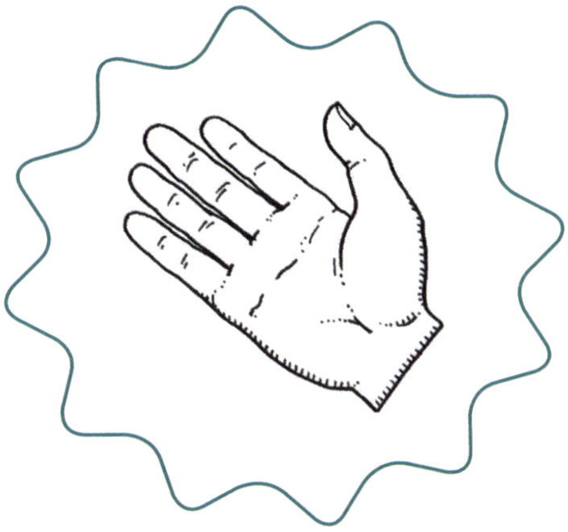

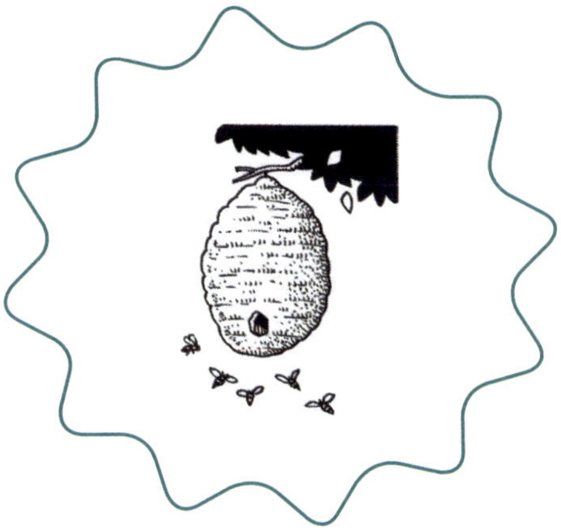

Handwriting

Track these letters

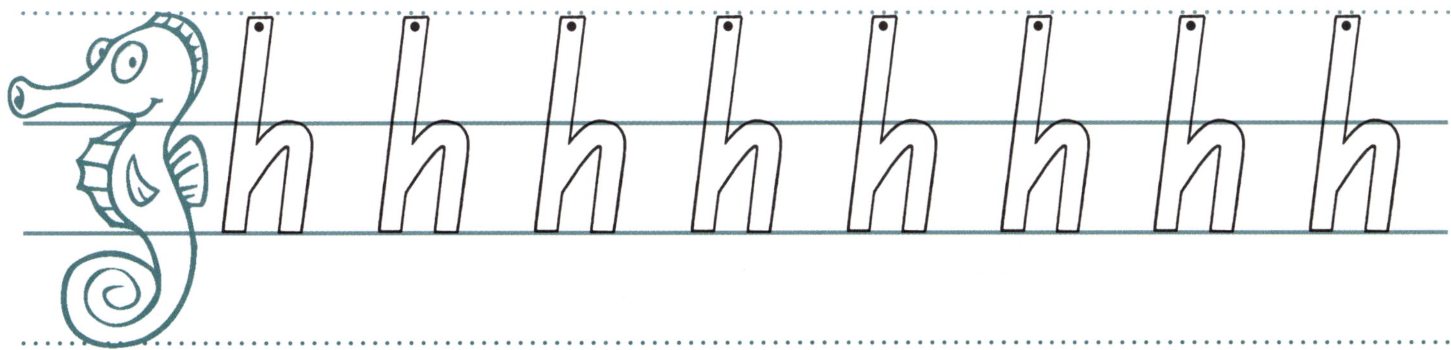

Trace these letters

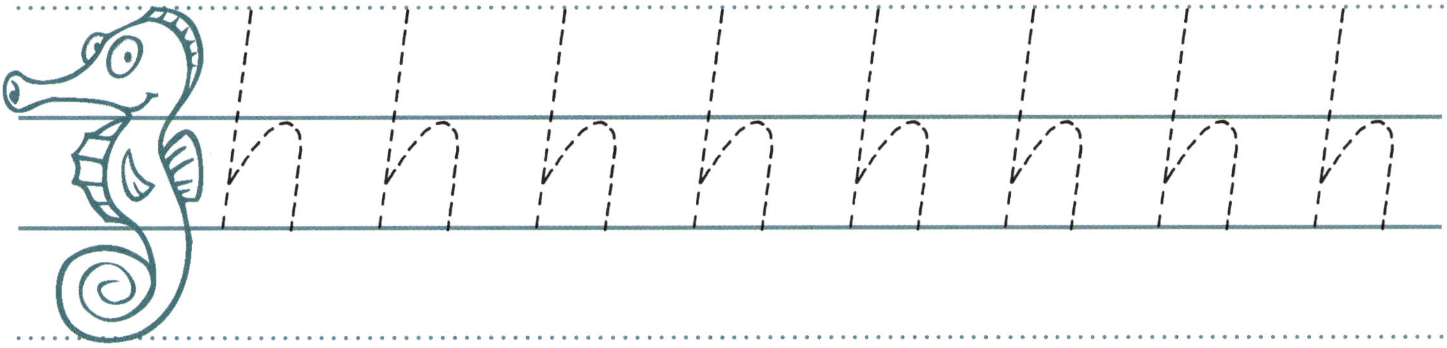

Aa Bb Cc Dd Ee Ff Gg Hh Ii Jj Kk Ll Mm Nn Oo Pp Qq Rr Ss Tt Uu Vv Ww Xx Yy Zz

Short vowel sound  e as in *elephant*

E e

Use this QR code to watch and listen to the **letter E** sound cards below

 elephant	 elf
  egg	 escalator

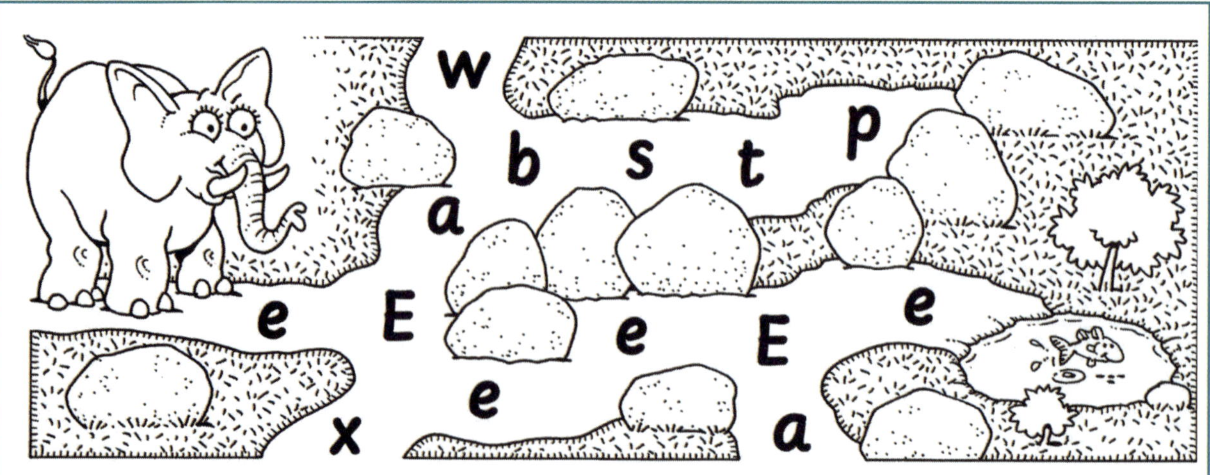

Ellie needs to find the path to the waterhole.
Follow the **Ee**s to help her.

  ISBN: 9781925726343

Short vowel sound e as in *elephant*

Say the names of the pictures below.
Colour pictures that begin with the letter 'e'.

Handwriting

Track these letters

Trace these letters

  ISBN: 9781925726343

Consonant sound  as in *rabbit*

Use this QR code to watch and listen to the **letter R** sound cards below

 rabbit	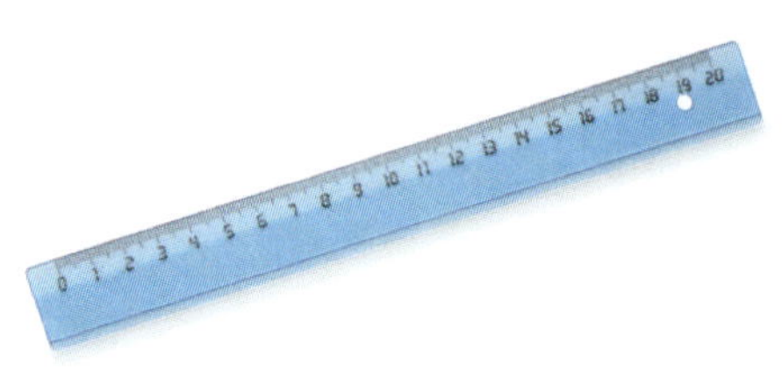 ruler
 ram	 rhino

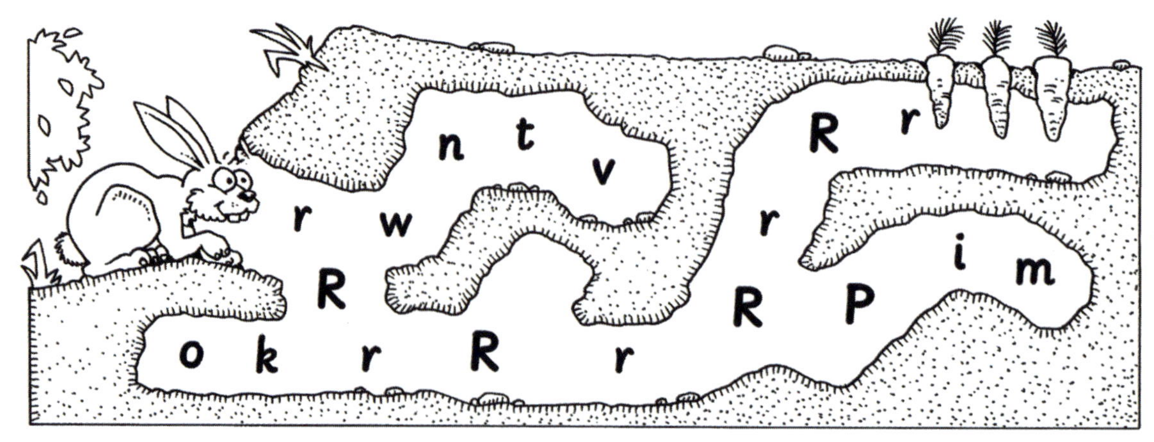

Help Rufus Rabbit find his favourite treat by drawing a path along the letter **Rr**s.

Consonant sound r as in *rabbit*

Say the names of the pictures below.
Colour pictures that begin with the letter 'r'.

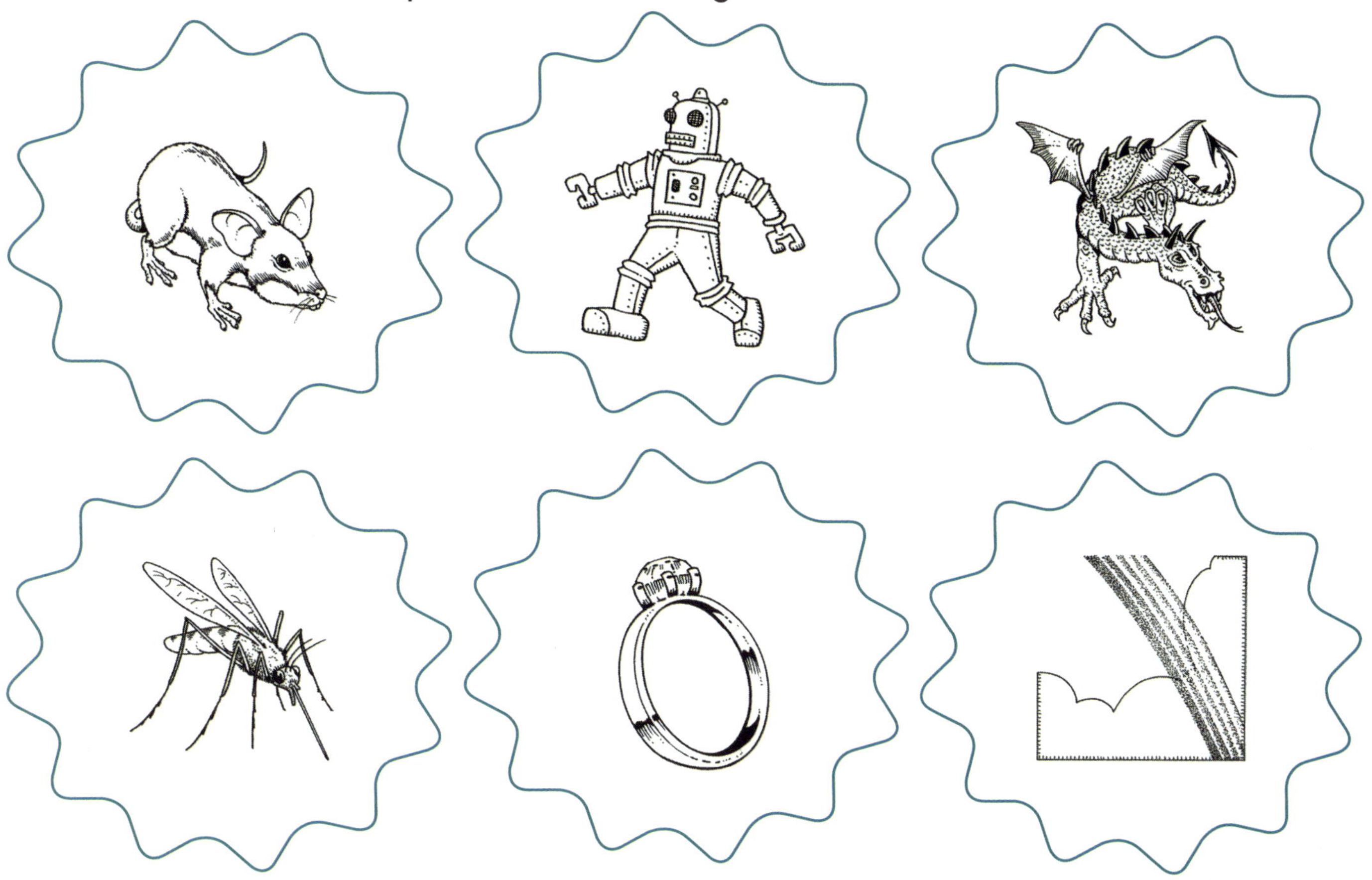

Handwriting

Track these letters

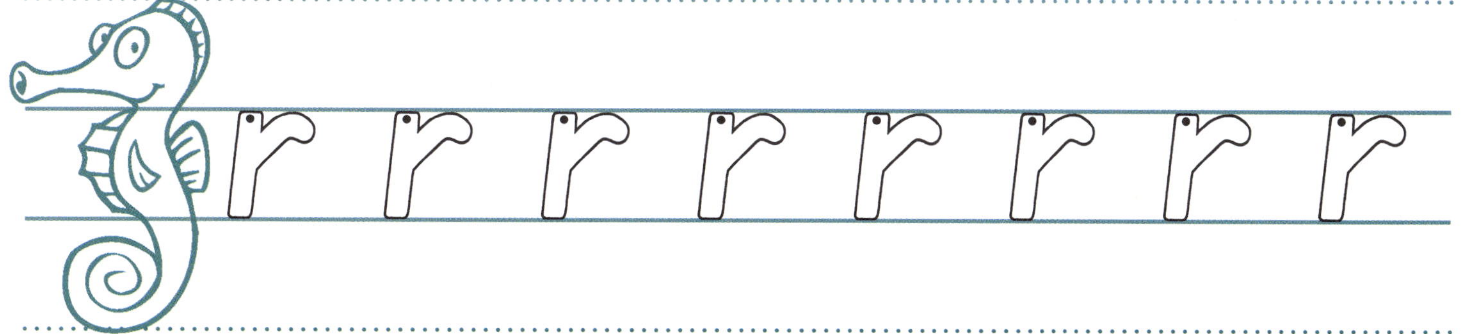

Trace these letters

  ISBN: 9781925726343

Aa Bb Cc Dd Ee Ff Gg Hh Ii Jj Kk Ll Mm Nn Oo Pp Qq Rr Ss Tt **Uu** Vv Ww Xx Yy Zz

Short vowel sound as in *umbrella*

U u

Use this QR code to watch and listen to the **letter U** sound cards below

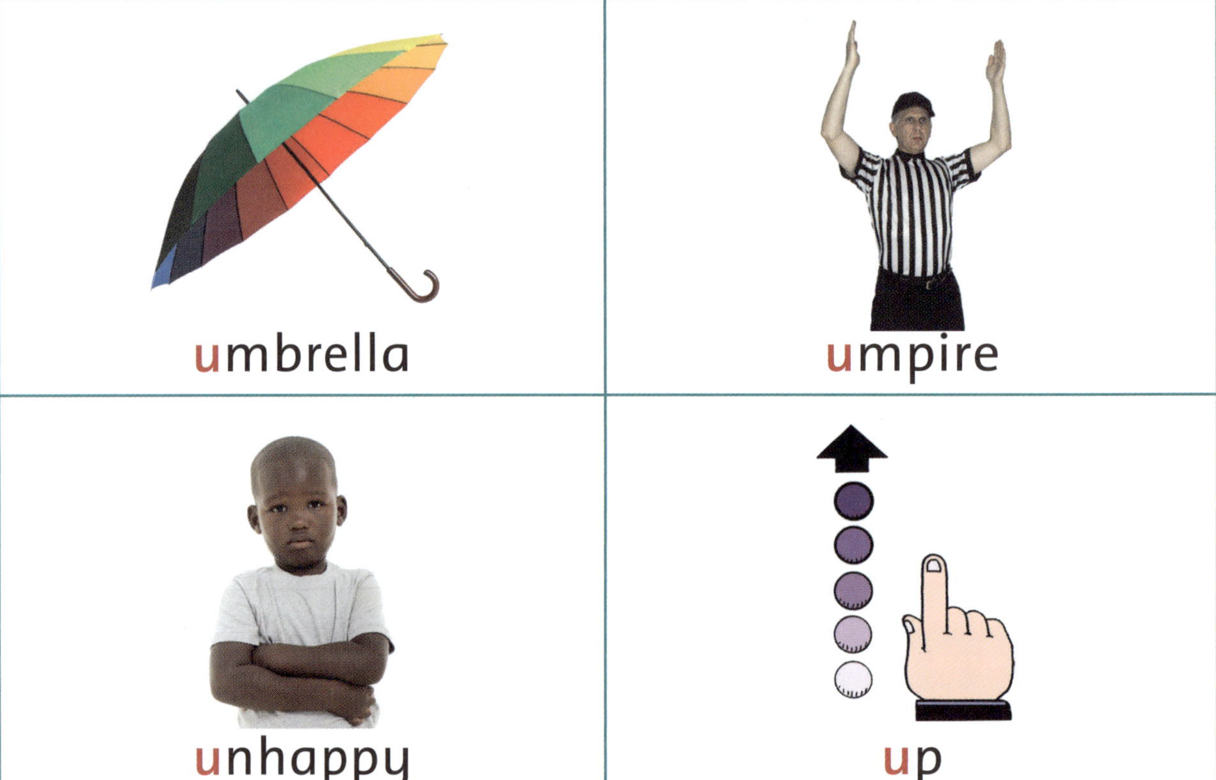

Circle and count the letter **Uus** falling down like rain on the umbrellas.

ISBN: 9781925726343

Short vowel sound u as in *umbrella*

Say the names of the pictures below.
Colour pictures that begin with the letter ‘u’.

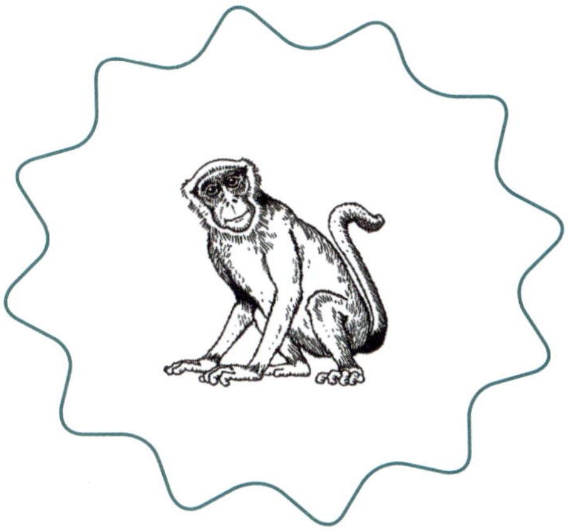

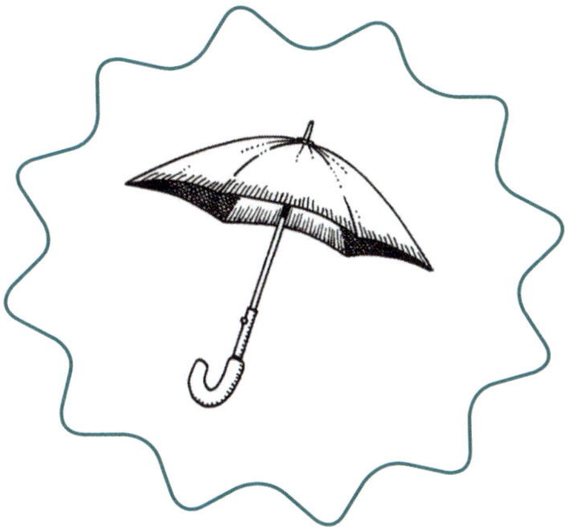

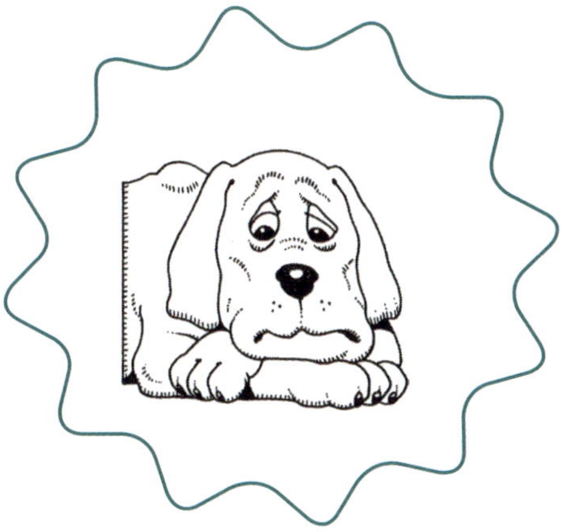

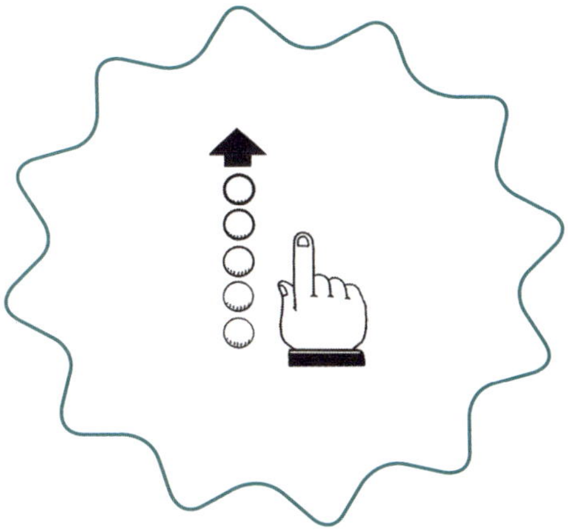

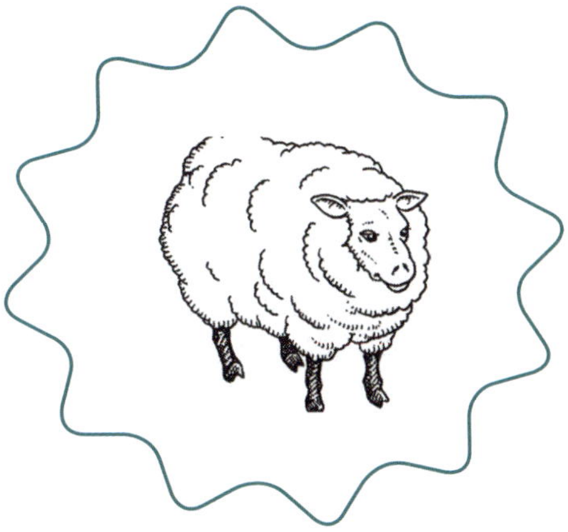

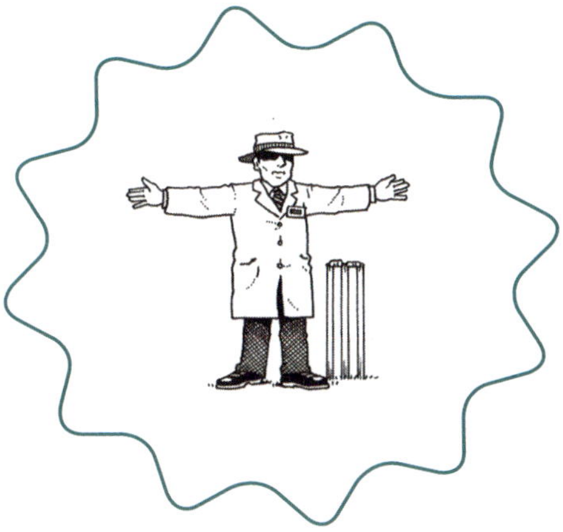

Handwriting

Track these letters

u u u u u u u u

Trace these letters

u u u u u u u u

  ISBN: 9781925726343

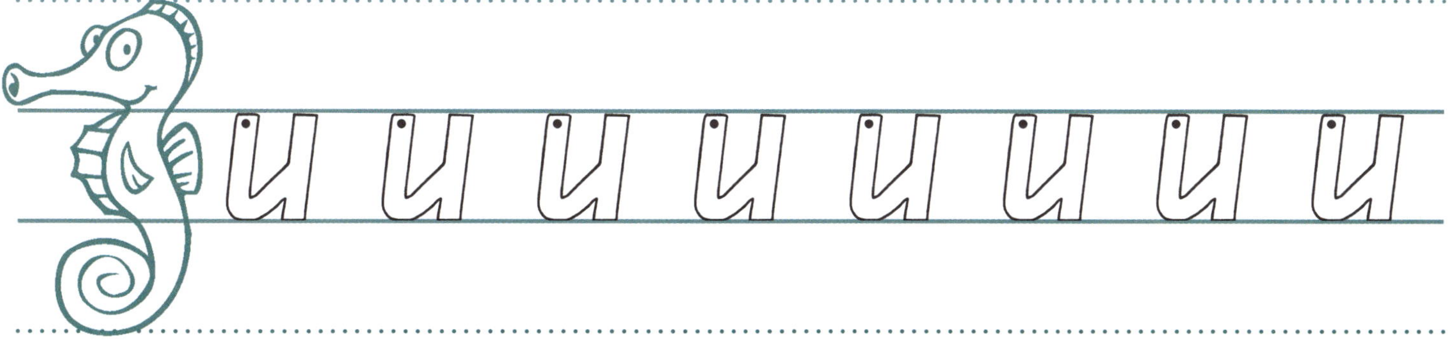

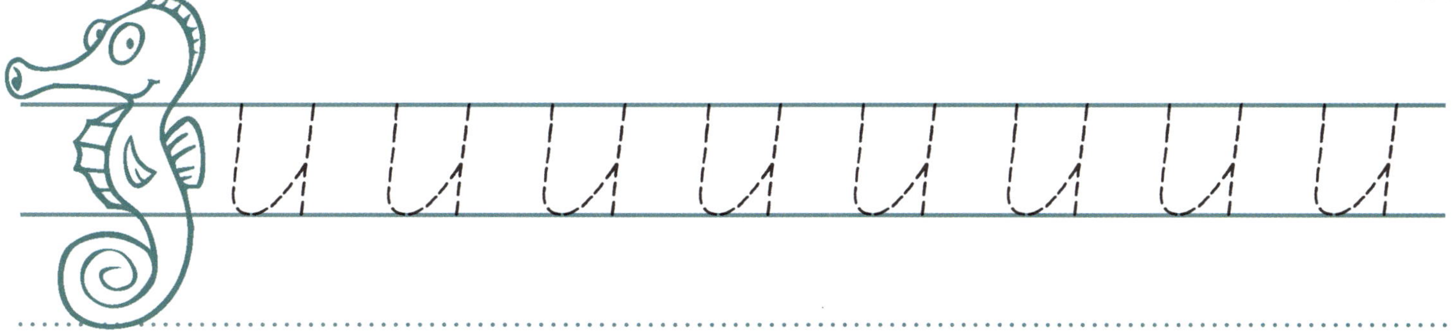

Aa Bb Cc Dd Ee Ff Gg Hh Ii Jj Kk Ll Mm Nn Oo Pp Qq Rr Ss Tt Uu Vv Ww Xx Yy Zz

⋆ Review ⋆

Say the names of the pictures below. Draw a circle around the beginning sound.

Say the names of the pictures below. Write the beginning sound.

  ISBN: 9781925726343

Decoding

Now you know these letters and sounds: s a t p i n d m g o c b h e r u
You can blend them to make and read these words.

Say the sounds	Blend the sounds	Read the word
Point to each letter as you say the sound.	Slide your finger from one sound to the next as you say the sound.	Point to the word as you read it.
h u g	h u g	hug
h u m	h u m	hum
r u b	r u b	rub
r e d	r e d	red
c u b	c u b	cub
t e n	t e n	ten
h i m	h i m	him
b u t	b u t	but
r o t	r o t	rot
r i g	r i g	rig

Read the words. Draw lines to match them to the pictures.

ham

bus

bug

hen

rat

hut

cup

bed

 © PASCAL PRESS ISBN: 9781925726343

Spelling

Now you can read these words, you can write them too.

Trace the words. Then write them on the lines below.

hat hop rag

grub best pet

mess hit cut

bend rug gum

Choose one of the letters you know to complete these words.
Read the words.

h__t __eg __ip

r__g cu__ r__st

  ISBN: 9781925726343

Spelling

Say the names of the pictures below.
Stretch out the word to hear the beginning,
middle and end sound. Write the words on the lines below.

  ISBN: 9781925726343

High frequency words – Set 3

Learn these words.

has	have	to	said	like

Comprehension

Read the sentences. Draw a picture to match.

I see a pup. The pup is in the tent.	I cut my hand. I ran to mum. Mum said I must rest.

The red hen has an egg in a big nest.	I have a pet bug. My pet bug can hop. I like my pet bug.

  ISBN: 9781925726343

Comprehension

Look at the pictures. Read the sentences. Write in the missing word.

I am in a

___ ___ ___ ___

at the camp.

The pet dog

___ ___ ___

to the man.

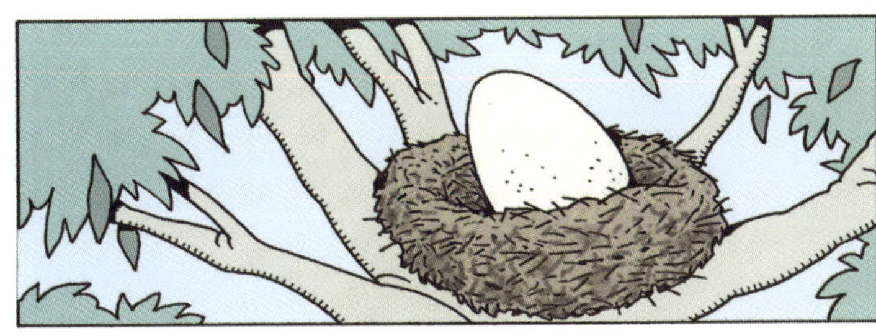

Here is a big egg

in a ___ ___ ___ ___.

This sentence is jumbled. Write it correctly on the lines below.

rug. big The bug red on the sat

  ISBN: 9781925726343

Consonant sound  as in *fish*

Ff

Use this QR code to watch and listen to the letter F sound cards below

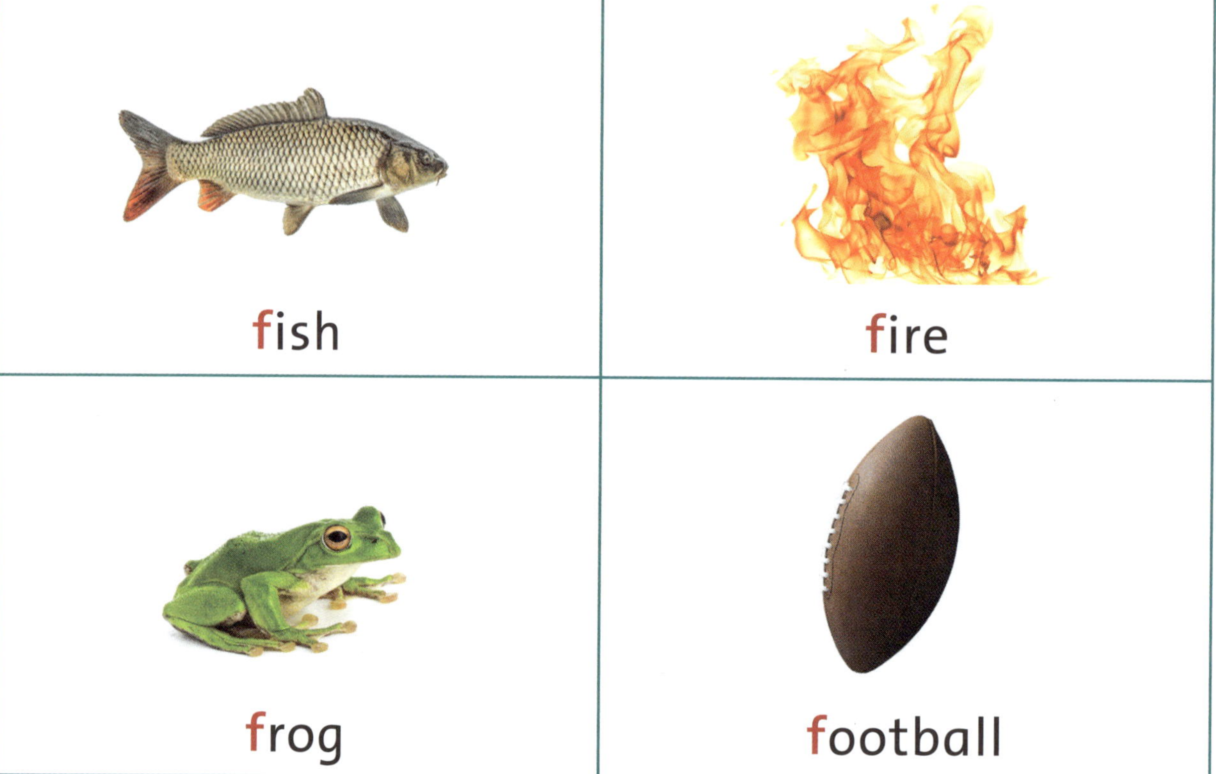

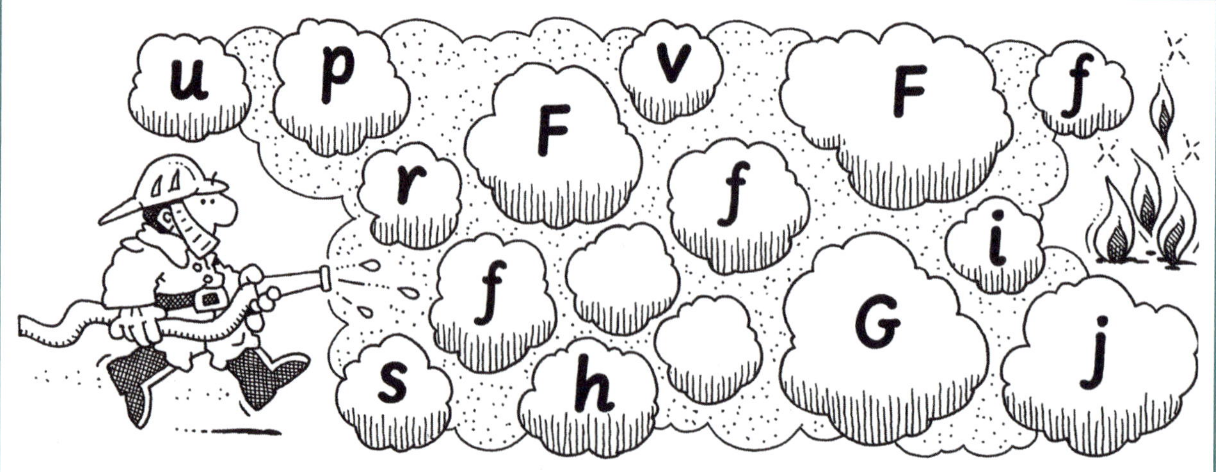

Fireman Fred needs to follow the **Ff**s to get to the fire quickly. Show him the way.

  ISBN: 9781925726343

Consonant sound f as in *fish*

Say the names of the pictures below.
Colour the pictures that begin with the letter 'f'.

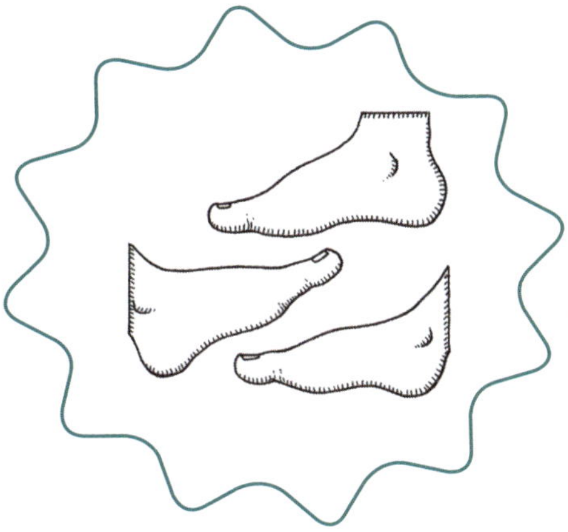

Handwriting

Track these letters

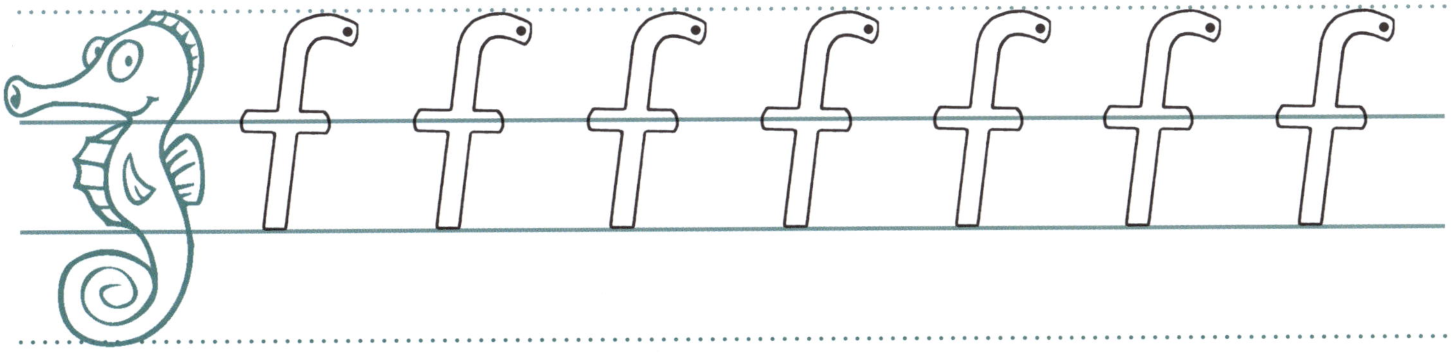

Trace these letters

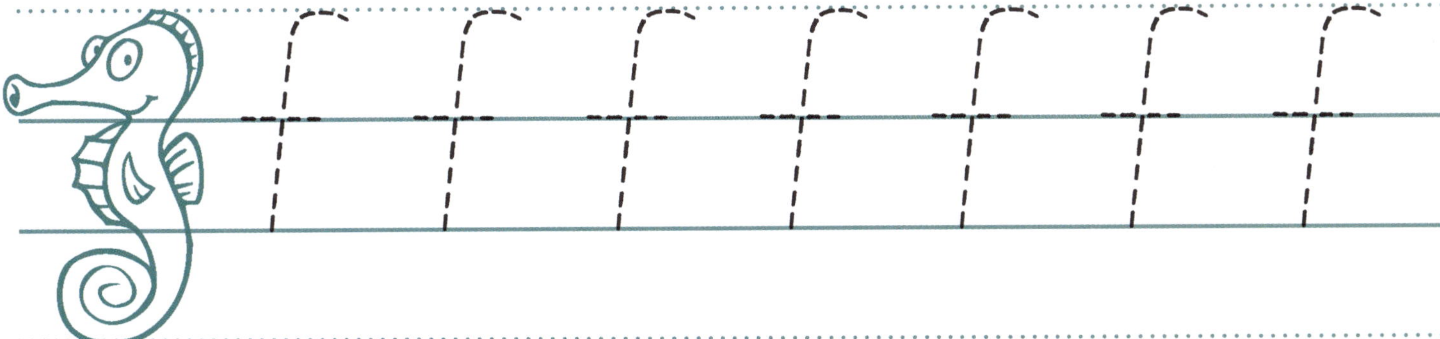

  ISBN: 9781925726343

Aa
Bb
Cc
Dd
Ee
Ff
Gg
Hh
Ii
Jj
Kk
Ll
Mm
Nn
Oo
Pp
Qq
Rr
Ss
Tt
Uu
Vv
Ww
Xx
Yy
Zz

Consonant sound  as in *lion*

Use this QR code to watch and listen to the letter L sound cards below

 lion	 leaf
 ladder	 lemon

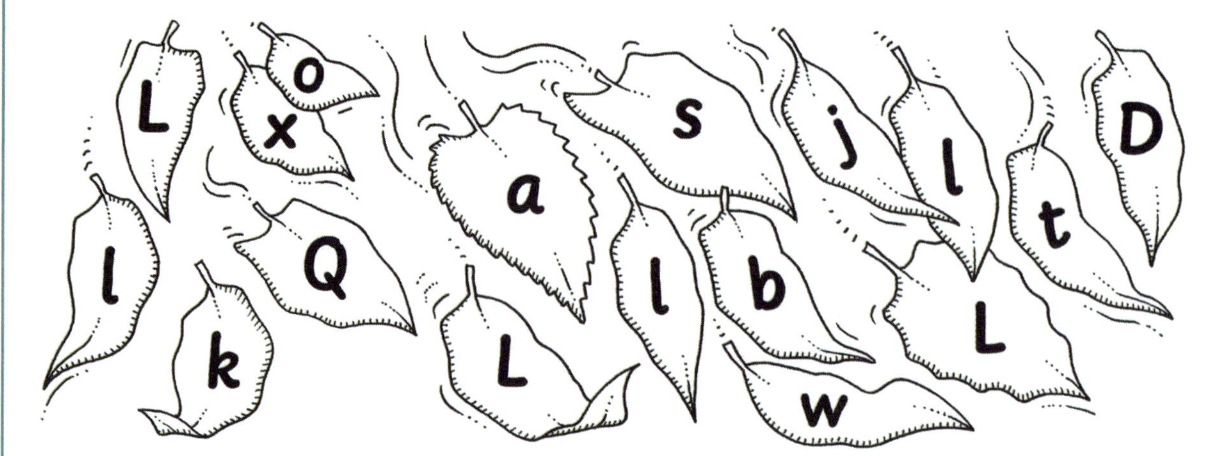

Lots of different leaves falling. Colour them all yellow except for **Ll** ones.

Consonant sound l as in *lion*

Say the names of the pictures below.
Colour the pictures that begin with the letter 'l'.

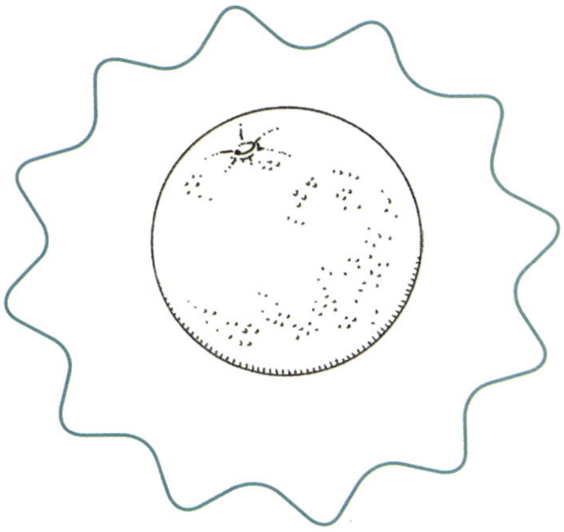

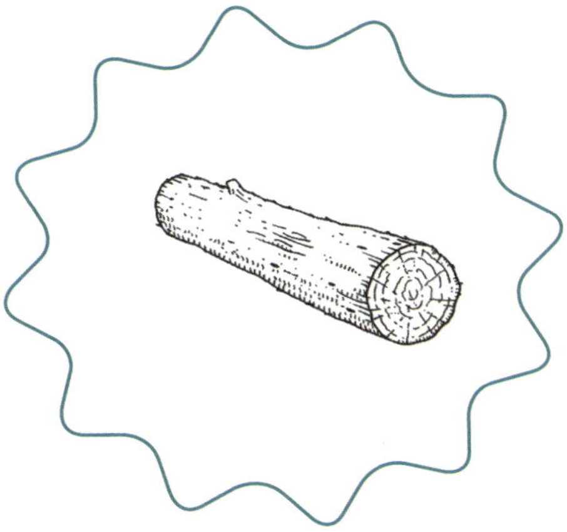

Handwriting

Track these letters

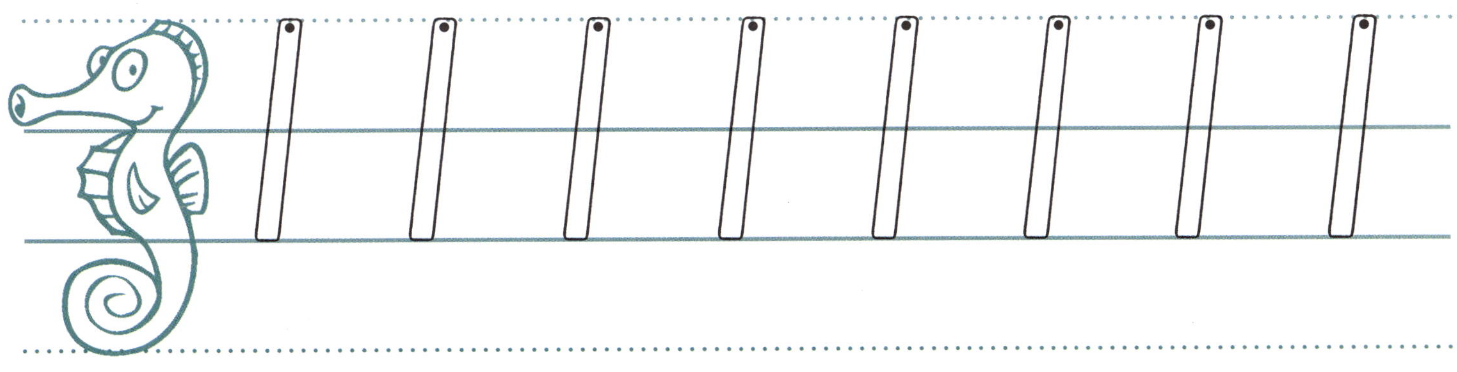

Trace these letters

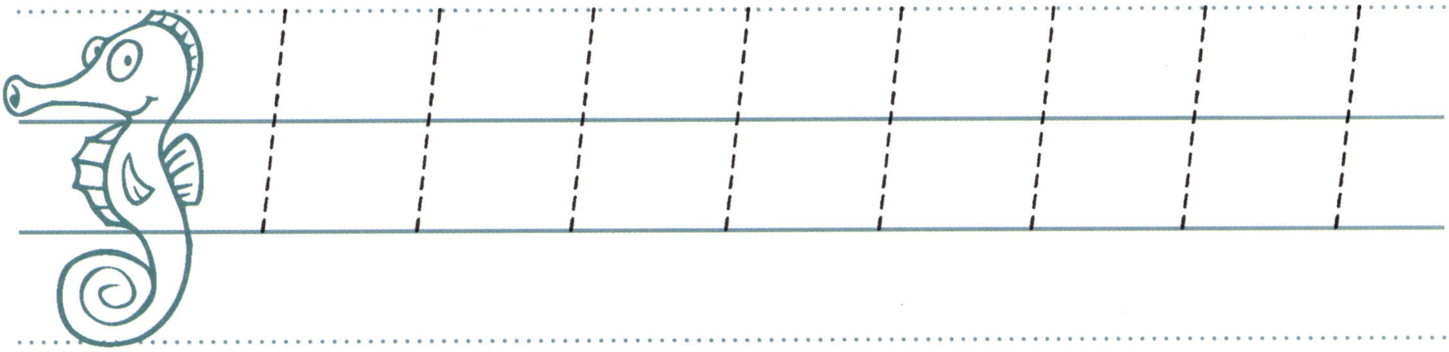

 © PASCAL PRESS ISBN: 9781925726343

Aa Bb Cc Dd Ee Ff Gg Hh Ii Jj Kk Ll Mm Nn Oo Pp Qq Rr Ss Tt Uu Vv Ww Xx Yy Zz

Consonant sound  as in *jellyfish*

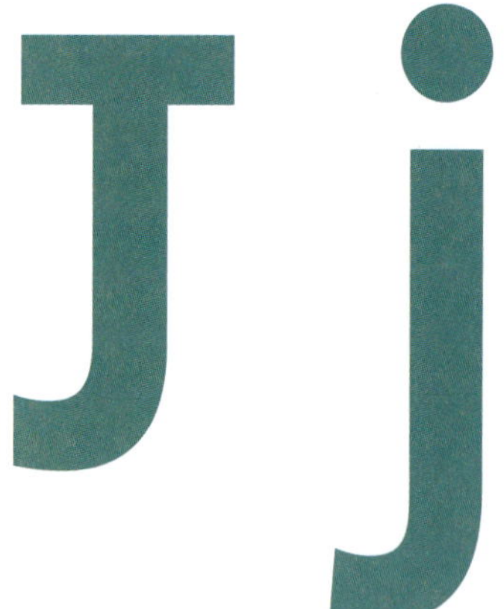

Use this QR code to watch and listen to the letter J sound cards below

 jellyfish	 jet
 jump	 juice

Jona is a jellyfish and juggles **Jj** shells.
Colour them for him.

  ISBN: 9781925726343

Consonant sound j as in *jellyfish*

Say the names of the pictures below.
Colour the pictures that begin with the letter 'j'.

Handwriting

Track these letters

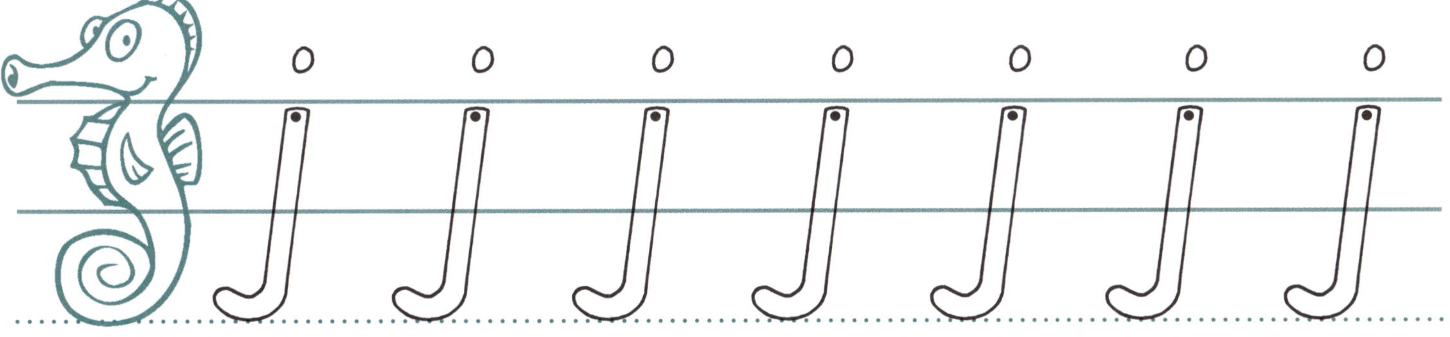

Trace these letters

  ISBN: 9781925726343

Aa Bb Cc Dd Ee Ff Gg Hh Ii Jj **Kk** Ll Mm Nn Oo Pp Qq Rr Ss Tt Uu Vv Ww Xx Yy Zz

Consonant sound  k as in *kangaroo*

Use this QR code to watch and listen to the letter K sound cards below

kangaroo

king

kitten

key

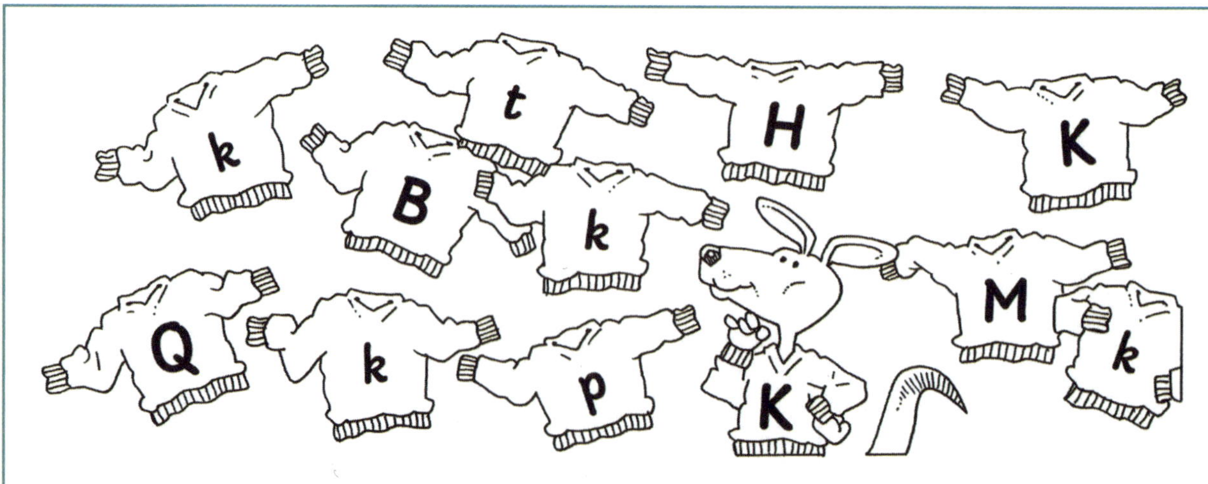

How many **Kk** jumpers has Kip Kangaroo got?
Colour them to find out.

  ISBN: 9781925726343

Consonant sound k as in *kangaroo*

Say the names of the pictures below.
Colour the pictures that begin with the letter 'k'.

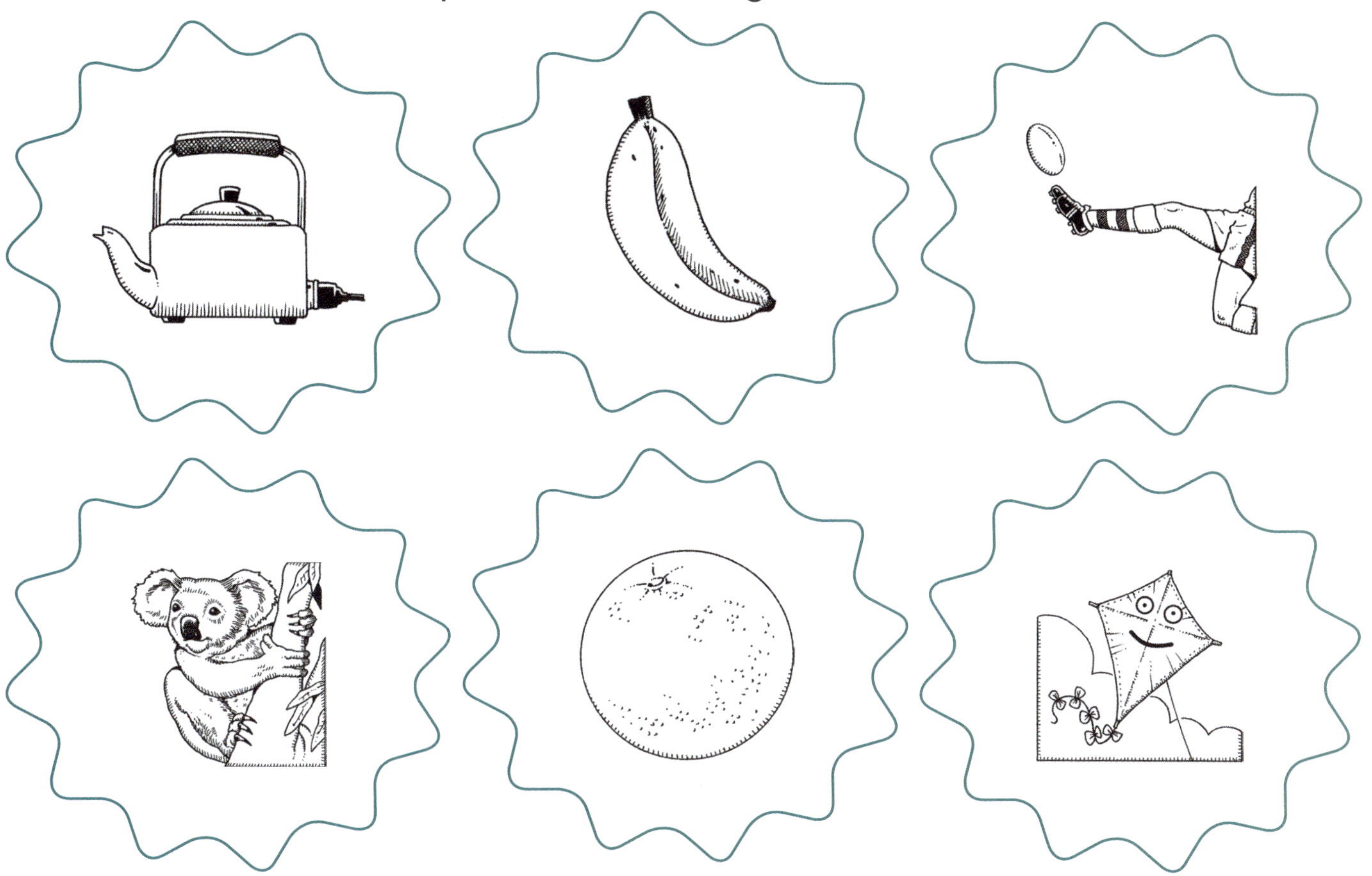

Handwriting

Track these letters

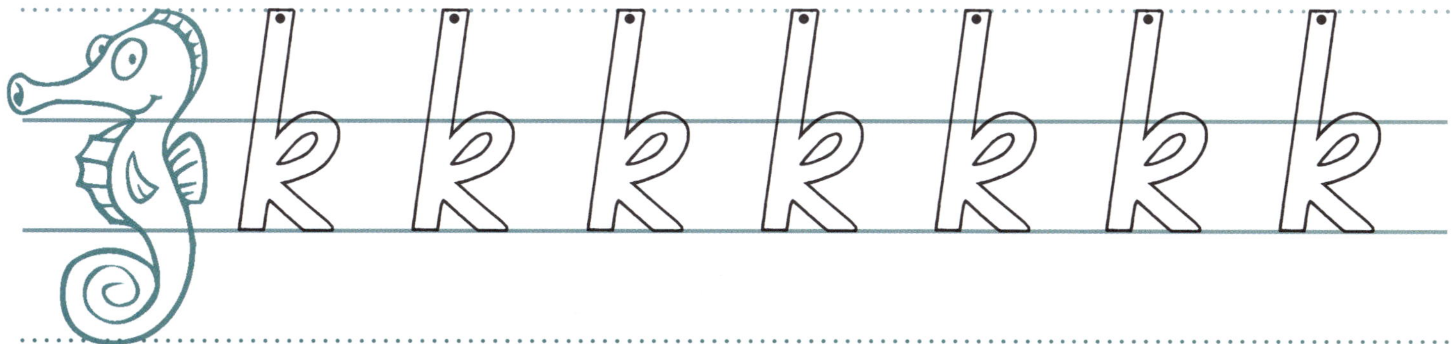

Trace these letters

  ISBN: 9781925726343

Aa Bb Cc Dd Ee Ff Gg Hh Ii Jj Kk Ll Mm Nn Oo Pp Qq Rr Ss Tt Uu Vv Ww Xx Yy Zz

★ Review ★

Say the names of the pictures below. Draw a circle around the sound you hear at the beginning of each word.

Say the names of the pictures below. Write the beginning sound.

Say the names of the pictures below. Draw a circle around the end sound.

  ISBN: 9781925726343

Decoding

Now you know these letters and sounds: s a t p i n d m g o c b h e u r f l j k

You can blend them to make and read these words.

Tricky!

We often use the letters 'c' and 'k' together to spell the 'k' sound at the end of a word, like in 'duck'.
We often use 'll' to spell the 'l' sound at the end of a word, like in 'well'.

Say the sounds	Blend the sounds	Read the word
Point to each letter as you say the sound.	Slide your finger from one sound to the next as you say the sound.	Point to the word as you read it.
f a n	f a n	fan
l a p	l a p	lap
k i t	k i t	kit
j a m	j a m	jam
d u ck	d u ck	duck
f e ll	f e ll	fell
o ff	o ff	off

Read the words. Draw lines to match them to the pictures.

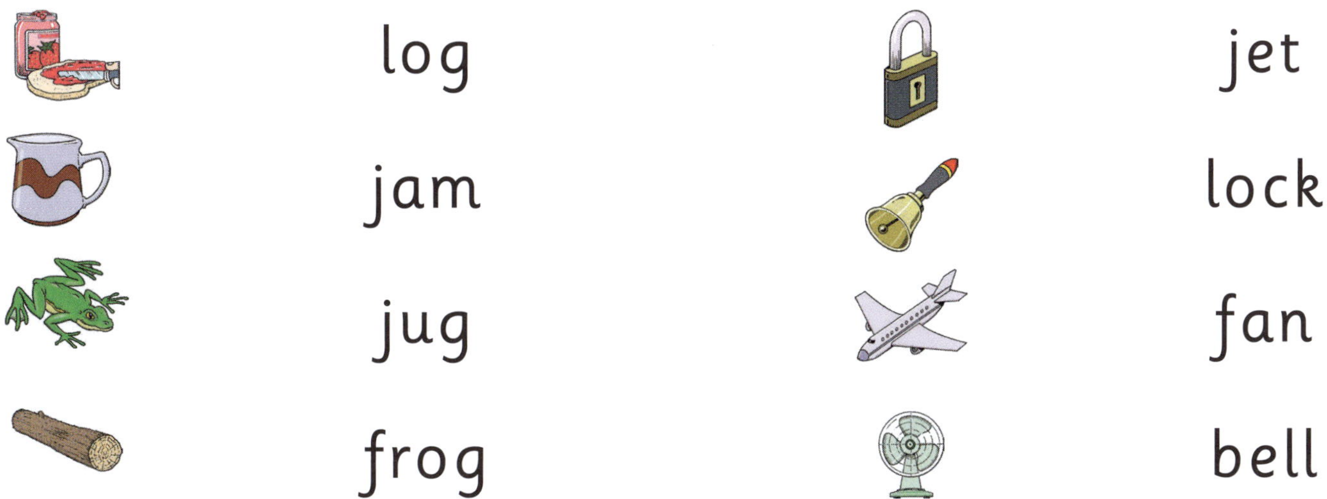

  ISBN: 9781925726343

Spelling

Now you can read these words, you can write them too.

Trace the words. Then write them on the lines below.

fog lap jab

kit off fill

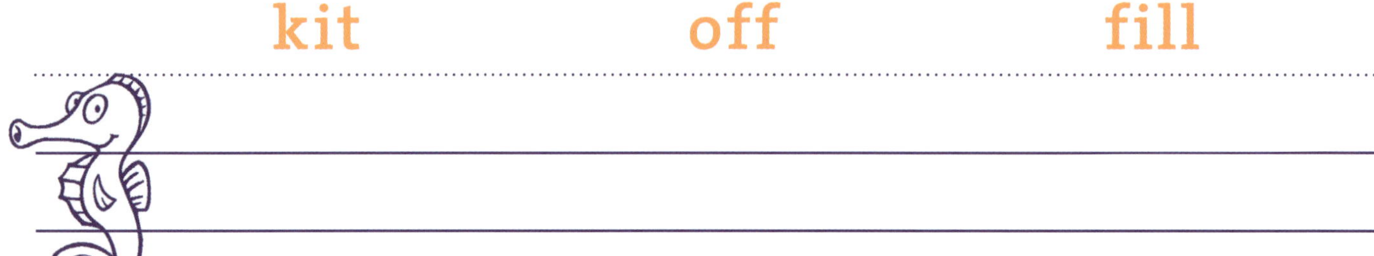

duck Jack huff

lamp bell lend

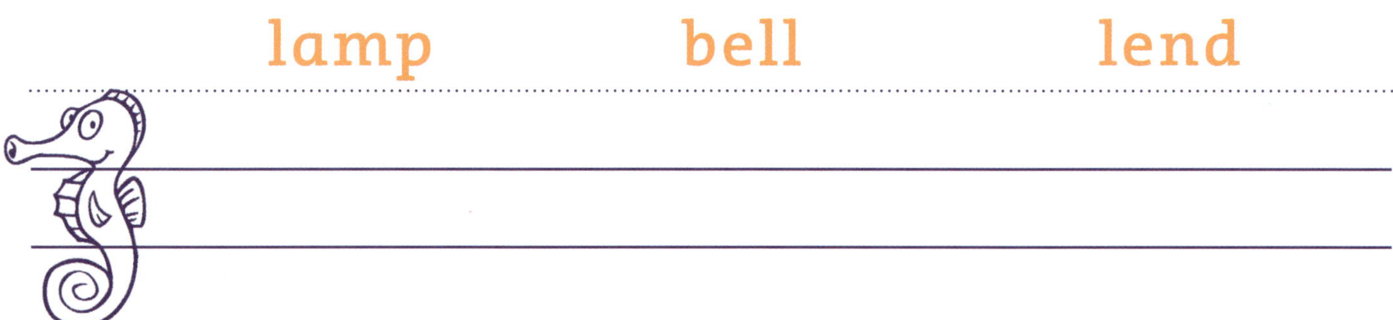

Choose letters you know to complete these words.
Read the words.

l__p __uck ja__

d__ll li__ __ock

  ISBN: 9781925726343

Spelling

Say the names of the pictures below.
Stretch out the word to hear the beginning,
middle and end sounds. Write the words on the lines below.

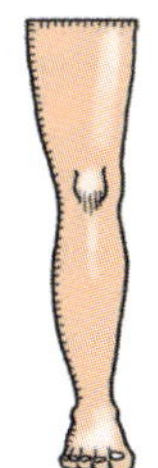

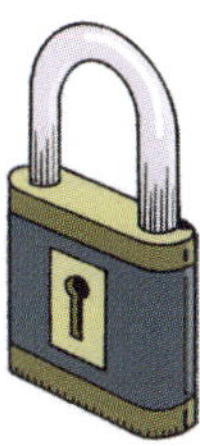

  ISBN: 9781925726343

High frequency words – Set 4

Learn these words.

you	me	are	go	down
You	too	with	little	come

Comprehension

Read the sentences. Draw a picture to match.

Look at the big truck. It can go down the hill.	See that little duck. It is on a log with a frog.

The pig and the frog are in the mud. The mud is wet.	I am in the mud. You can come and jump in the mud with me too.

  ISBN: 9781925726343

Comprehension

Look at the pictures. Read the sentences. Write in the missing word.

A __ __ __ __ __
is stuck in the mud.

The __ __ __ cat
has a red hat and
the little dog has a
__ __ __ __ __ cap.

Jack fell down the
__ __ __ __ and
hit his hand on a rock.

This sentence is jumbled. Write it correctly on the lines below.

and have I a sock sock. red black a

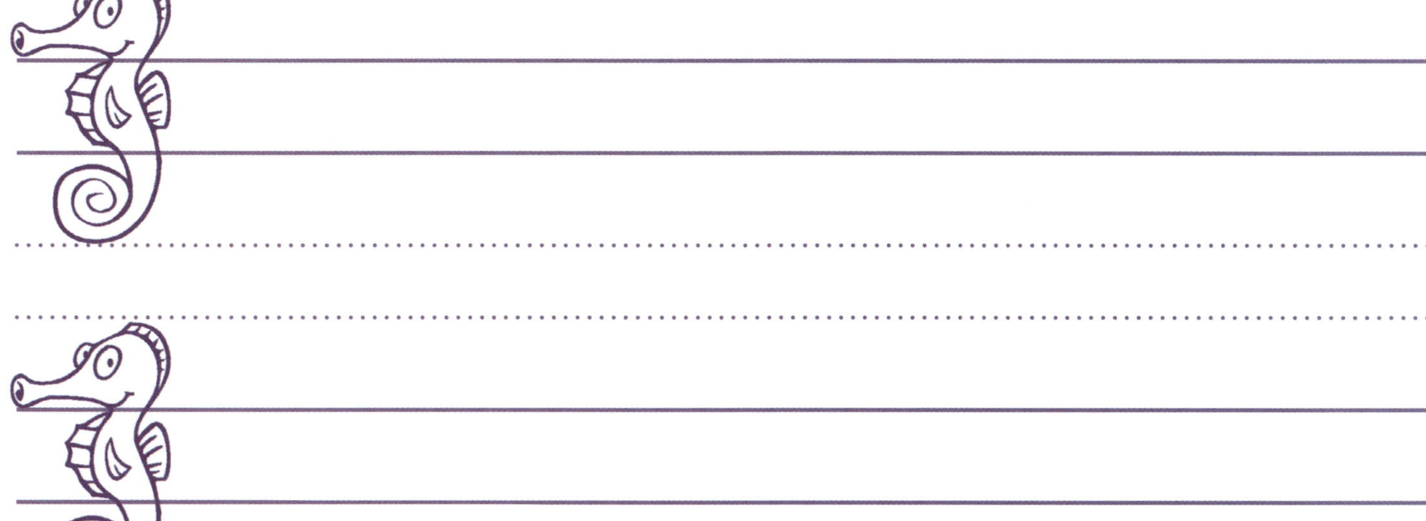

  ISBN: 9781925726343

Aa Bb Cc Dd Ee Ff Gg Hh Ii Jj Kk Ll Mm Nn Oo Pp Qq Rr Ss Tt Uu Vv Ww Xx Yy Zz

Consonant sound  v as in *vulture*

Use this QR code to watch and listen to the letter V sound cards below

 vulture	 vampire
 volcano	 vegetables

Vanessa sings the letter **Vv** loudest.
Colour them for her.

  ISBN: 9781925726343

Consonant sound **v** as in ***vulture***

Say the names of the pictures below.
Colour the pictures that begin with the letter 'v'.

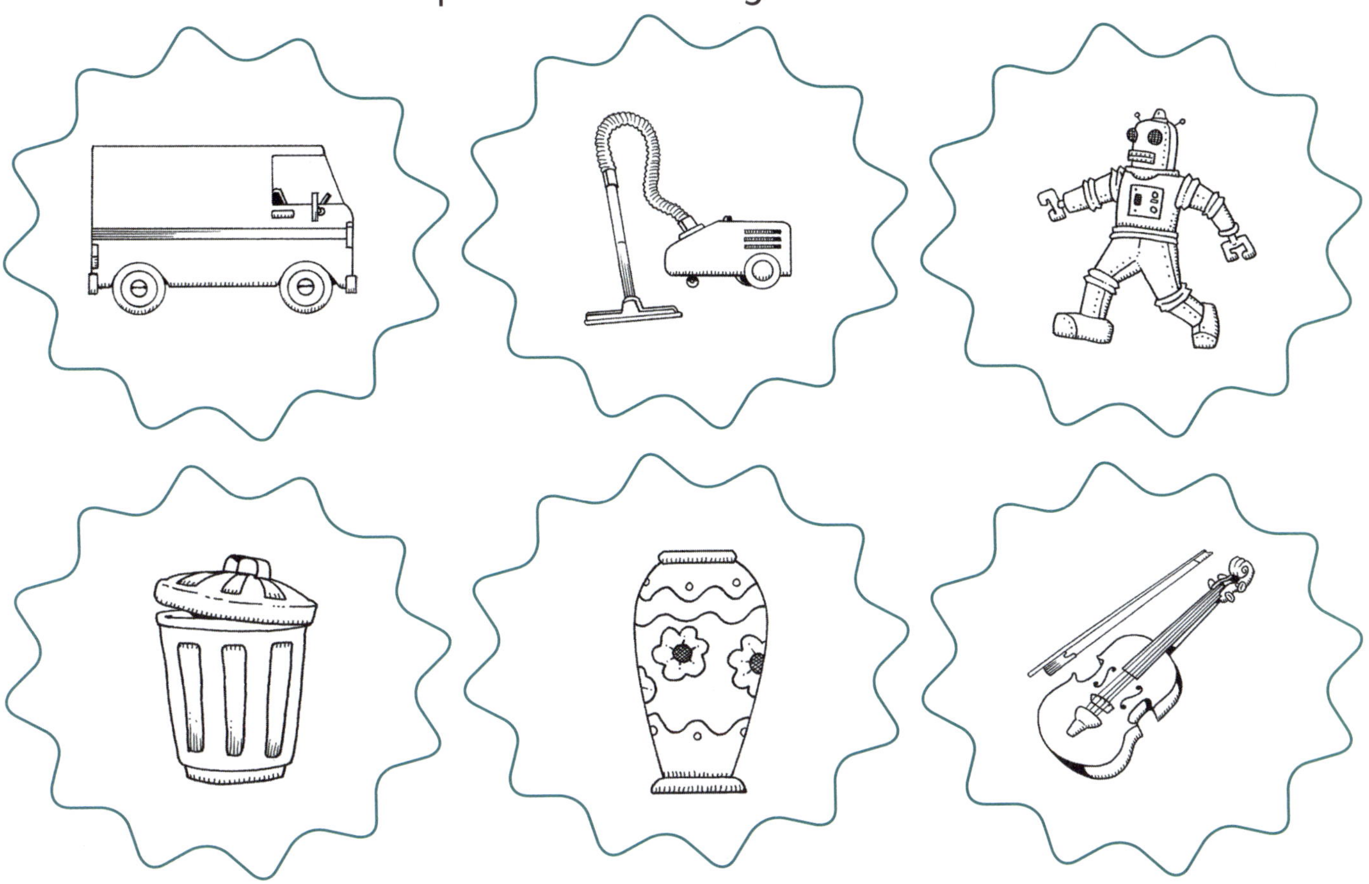

Handwriting

Track these letters

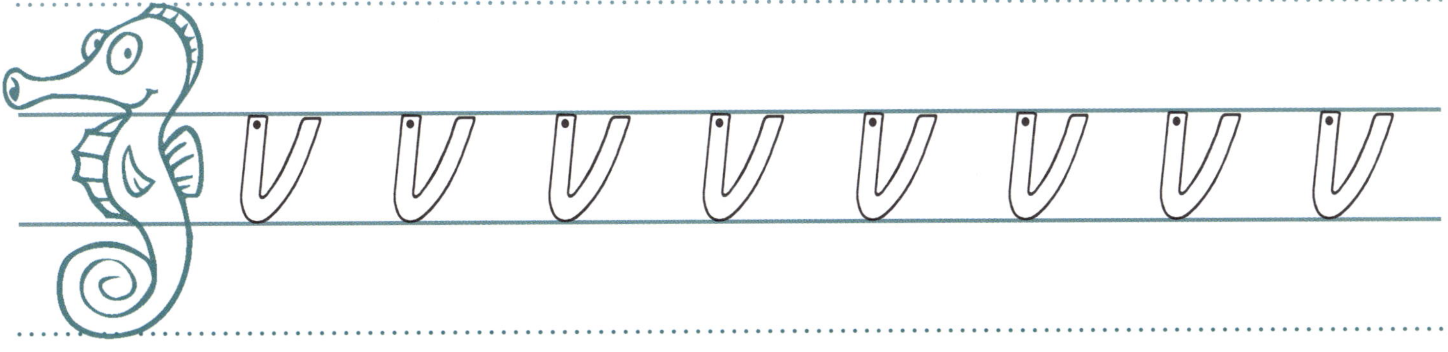

Trace these letters

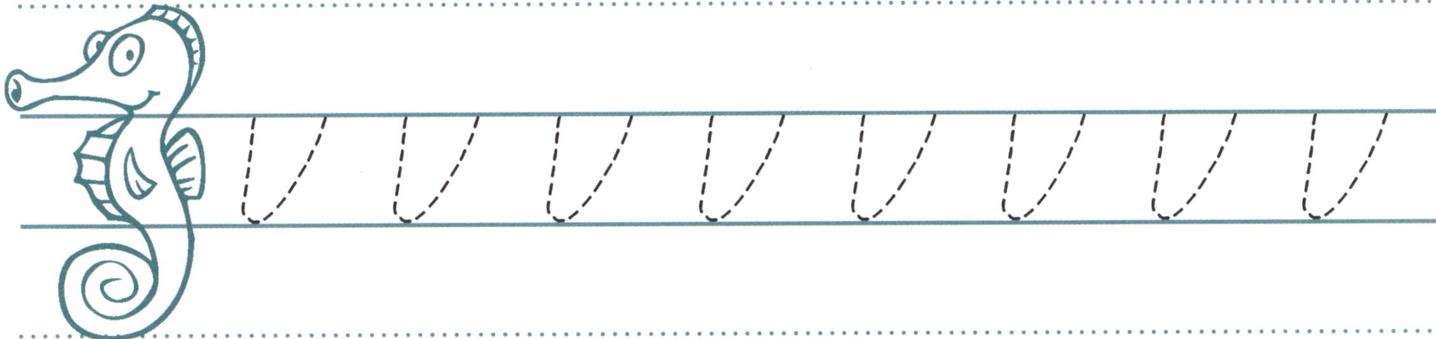

  ISBN: 9781925726343

Consonant sound W as in *walrus*

Use this QR code to watch and listen to the letter W sound cards below

walrus

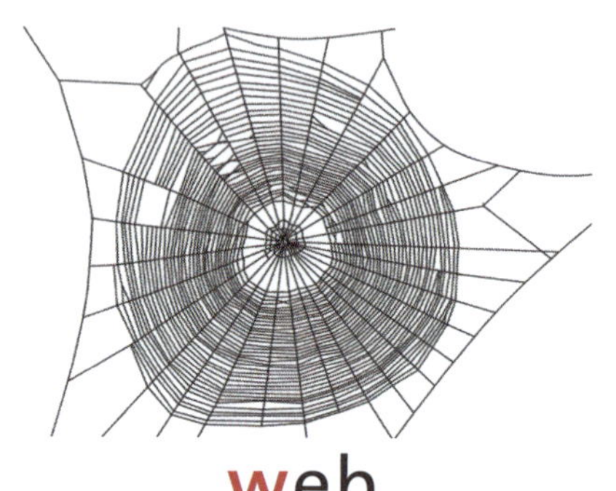

web

wolf

worm

Wendy and Wally Wagtail feed their chicks on the letter **Ww**. How many can you find? Circle them.

  ISBN: 9781925726343

Consonant sound w as in *walrus*

Say the names of the pictures below.
Colour the pictures that begin with the letter 'w'.

Handwriting

Track these letters

Trace these letters

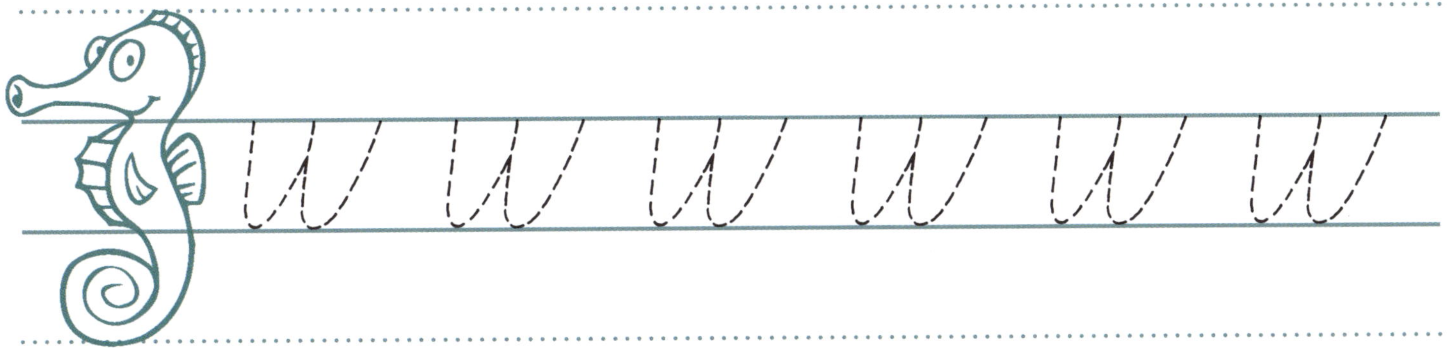

  ISBN: 9781925726343

Consonant sound  as in *yak*

Use this QR code to watch and listen to the letter Y sound cards below

 yak	 yoghurt
 yell	 yo-yo

The yoghurt van has spilled its load! Can you see how many **Ys** are in the yoghurt puddle? ☐

  ISBN: 9781925726343

Consonant sound y as in *yak*

Say the names of the pictures below.
Colour the pictures that begin with the letter 'y'.

Handwriting

Track these letters

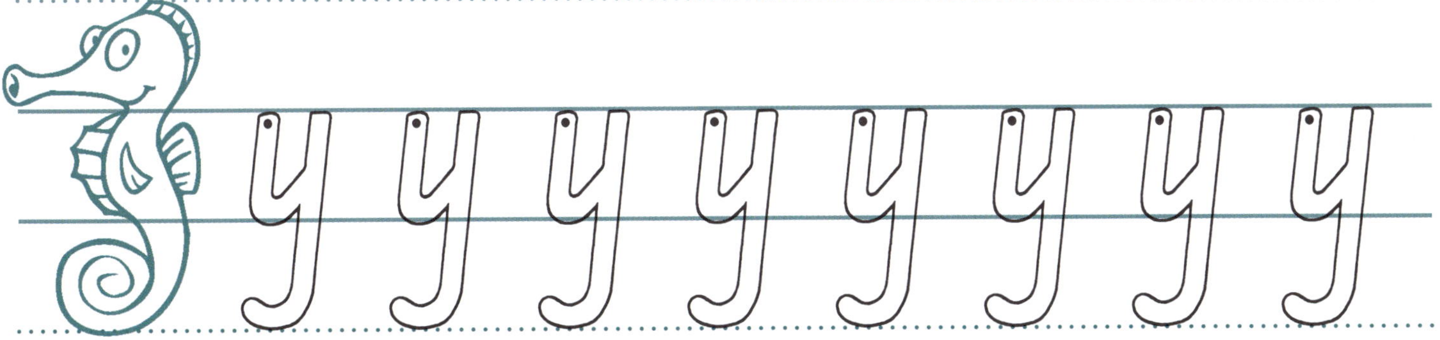

Trace these letters

  ISBN: 9781925726343

Consonant sound z as in *zebra*

Z z

Use this QR code to watch and listen to the letter Z sound cards below

 zebra	 zip
 zucchini	 zigzag

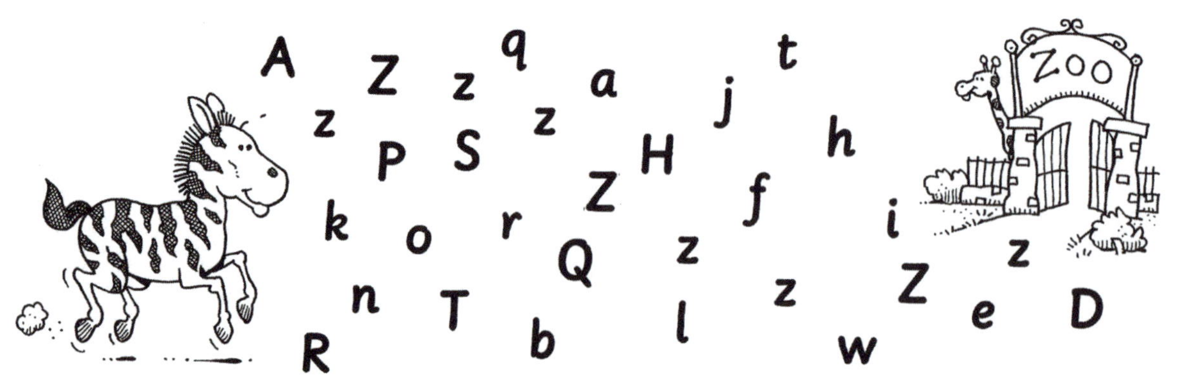

Zak is lost and must get back to the zoo. Show him the way by following the **Zz**s.

  ISBN: 9781925726343

Consonant sound z as in *zebra*

Say the names of the pictures below.
Colour the pictures that begin with the letter 'z'.

Handwriting

Track these letters

Trace these letters

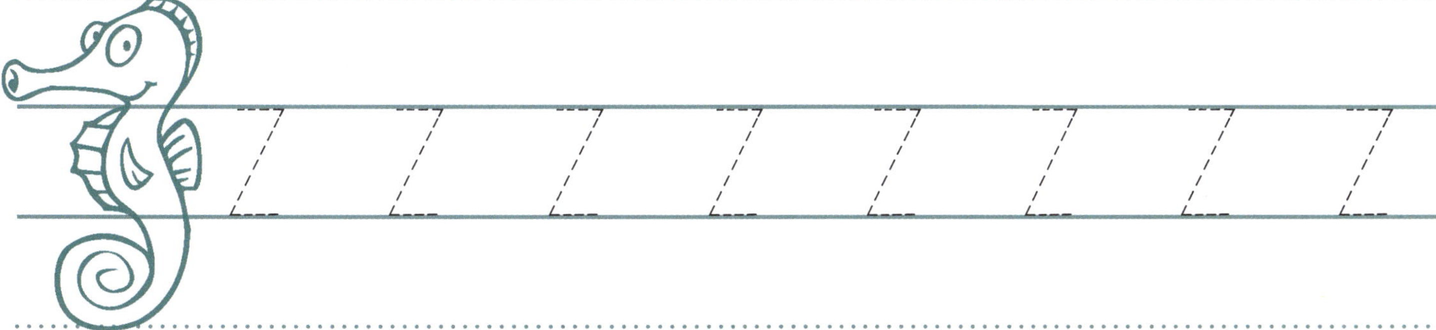

  ISBN: 9781925726343

Aa Bb Cc Dd Ee Ff Gg Hh Ii Jj Kk Ll Mm Nn Oo Pp Qq Rr Ss Tt Uu Vv Ww Xx Yy Zz

⋆ Review ⋆

Say the names of the pictures below. Draw a circle around the beginning sound.

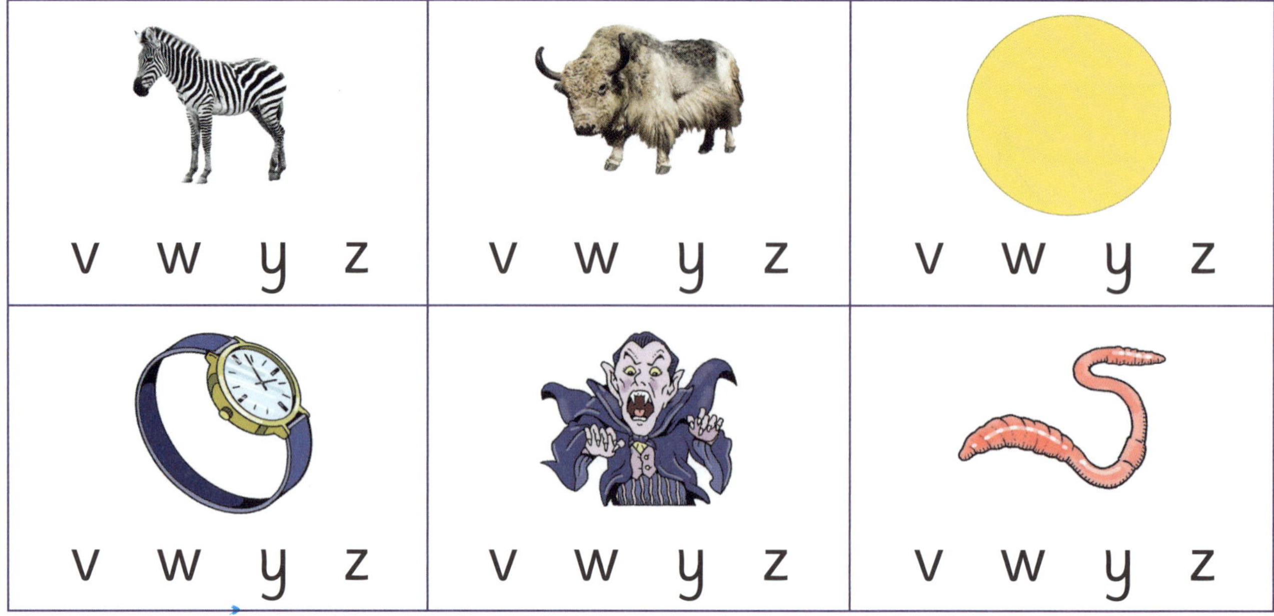

v w y z	v w y z	v w y z
v w y z	v w y z	v w y z

Say the names of the pictures below. Write the beginning sound of each word.

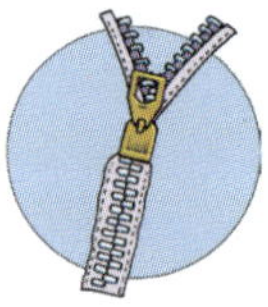

  ISBN: 9781925726343

Decoding

Now you know these letters and sounds: s a t p i n d m g o c b h e u r f l j k

You can blend them to make and read these words.

Tricky!
We often use 'zz' to spell the 'z' sound at the end of a word, like in 'buzz'.

Say the sounds	Blend the sounds	Read the word
Point to each letter as you say the sound.	Slide your finger from one sound to the next as you say the sound.	Point to the word as you read it.
v a n	v a n	van
w e t	w e t	wet
y a k	y a k	yak
z i p	z i p	zip
y u m	y u m	yum
b u zz	b u zz	buzz

Read the words. Draw lines to match them to the pictures.

yak

web

zip

van

vet

wig

well

yes

 © PASCAL PRESS ISBN: 9781925726343

Spelling

Now you can read these words, you can write them too.

Trace the words. Then write them on the lines below.

vat vet van

wet win wag

yam yum yes

zip zap zag

Choose letters you know to complete these words.
Read the words.

v__t __in zi__

w__ll ya__ __ap

  ISBN: 9781925726343

Spelling

Say the names of the pictures below.
Stretch out the word to hear the sound at the beginning, middle and end. Write the words on the lines below.

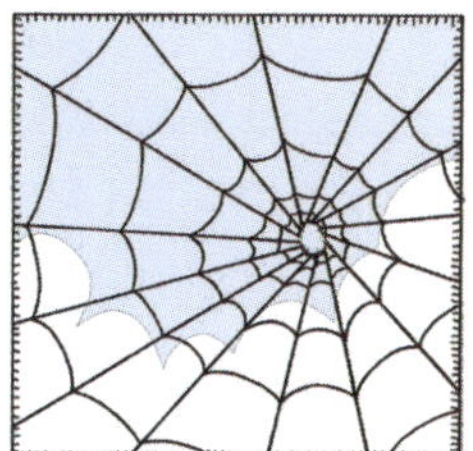

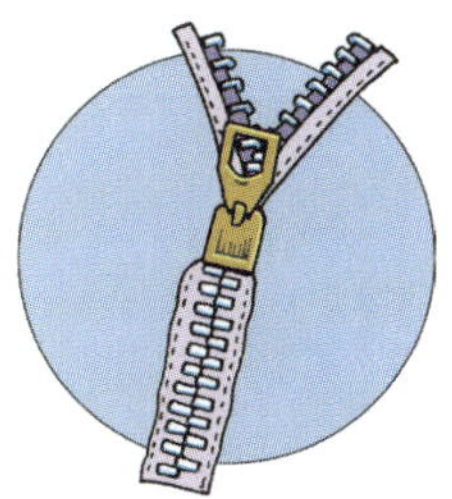

  ISBN: 9781925726343

High frequency words – Set 5

Learn these words.

we	no	where	some	going
We	No	Where	girl	boy

Comprehension

Read the sentences. Draw a picture to match.

Look at us. We are going down the hill in a big van.	The girl has a pet dog. The boy has some pet bugs.

Where are cats? The cats are on the well. Are the cats wet? No!	Look at my zip. My zip will not go up. My zip is stuck.

  ISBN: 9781925726343

Comprehension

Look at the pictures. Read the sentences. Write in the missing word.

This ___ ___ ___
has some jam. Yum!

This vet is stuck in
some ___ ___ ___
Yuck!

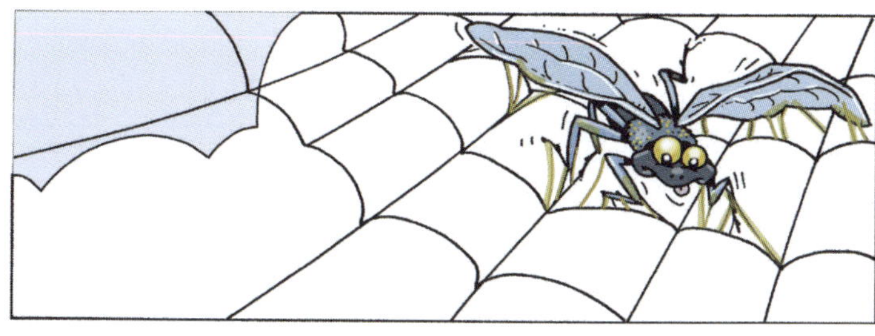

The bug went into
the ___ ___ ___.
Zap! It got stuck.

This sentence is jumbled. Write it correctly on the lines below.

hill The went yak down the

  ISBN: 9781925726343

Consonant sound  as in *quoll*

The letter 'q' is special because it's always accompanied by the letter 'u' as in 'queen'. It makes a sound like 'kw'.

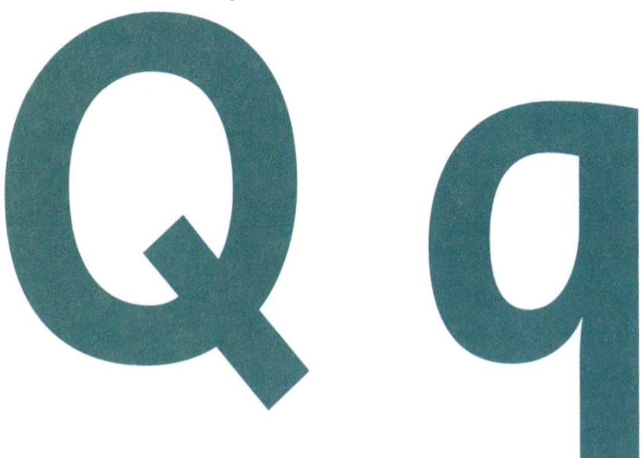

Use this QR code to watch and listen to the letter Q sound cards below

quoll

queen

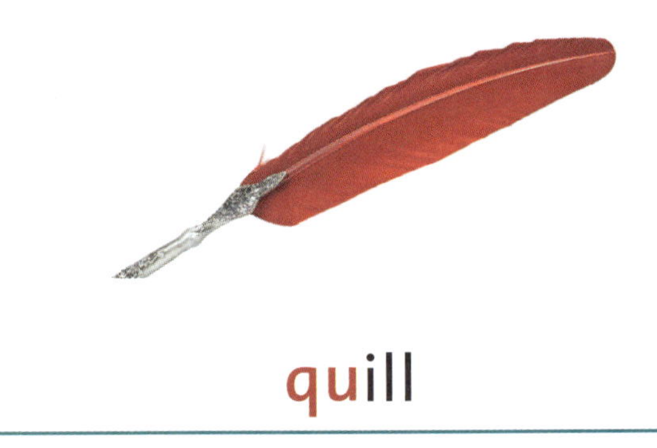

quill

quail

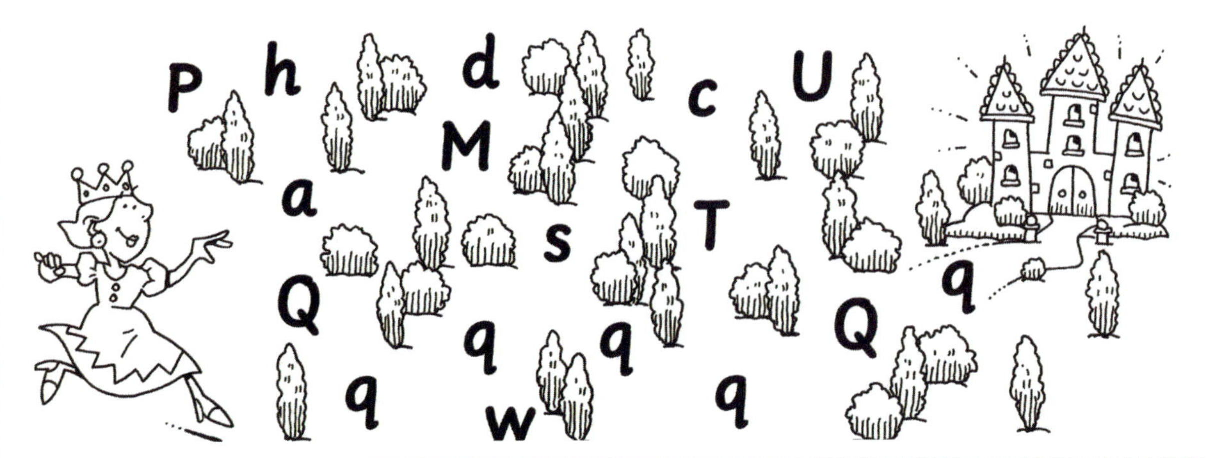

Find Queenie's short cut to the palace by drawing a path for her along the letter **Qq**s.

  ISBN: 9781925726343

Consonant sound q as in *quoll*

Say the names of the pictures below.
Colour the pictures that begin with the letter 'q'.

Handwriting

Track these letters

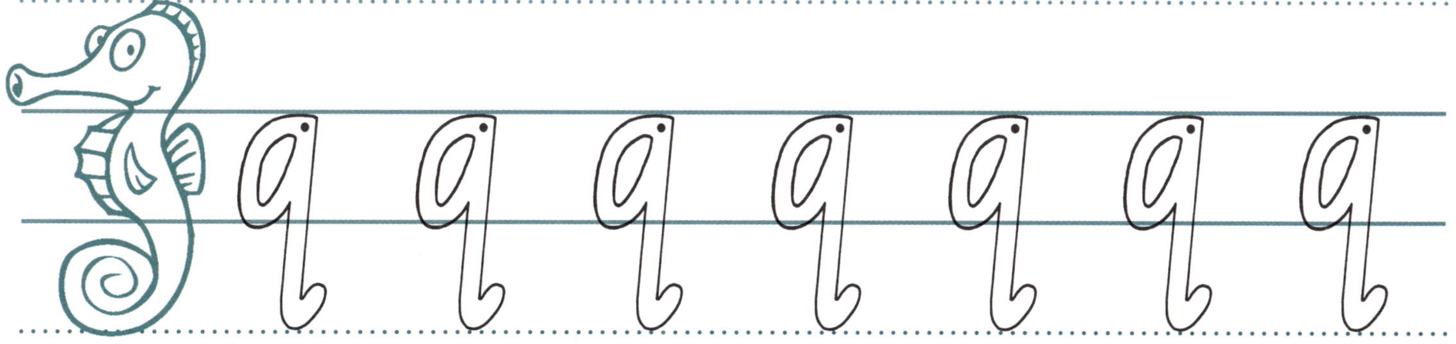

Trace these letters

  ISBN: 9781925726343

Aa Bb Cc Dd Ee Ff Gg Hh Ii Jj Kk Ll Mm Nn Oo Pp Qq Rr Ss Tt Uu Vv Ww **Xx** Yy Zz

Consonant sound  as in *fox*

The letter ‘x’ is special because it doesn’t often occur at the beginning of a word. It is usually in the middle or at the end of a word as in ’box’. It makes a sound like ‘ks’.

Use this QR code to watch and listen to the letter X sound cards below

 fox	 box
 mix	 six

Xavier the pirate has buried 5 lots of treasure under the letter Xxs. Can you find them all?

Consonant sound x as in *fox*

Say the names of the pictures below.
Colour the pictures that begin with the letter 'x'.

Tricky!
When 'x' is at the begining of a word it often has the sound 'z' as in Xavier and Xylophone.

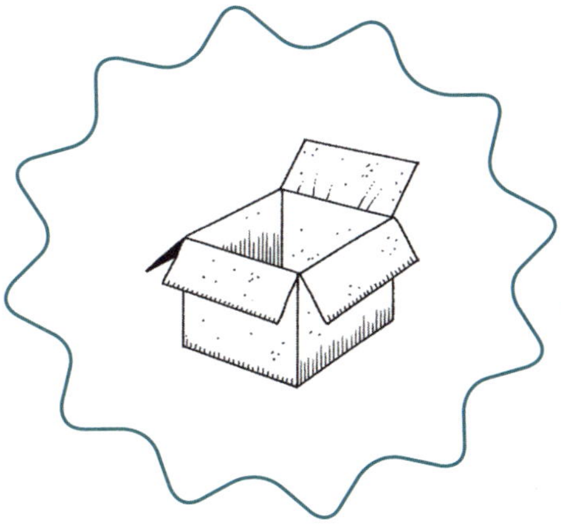

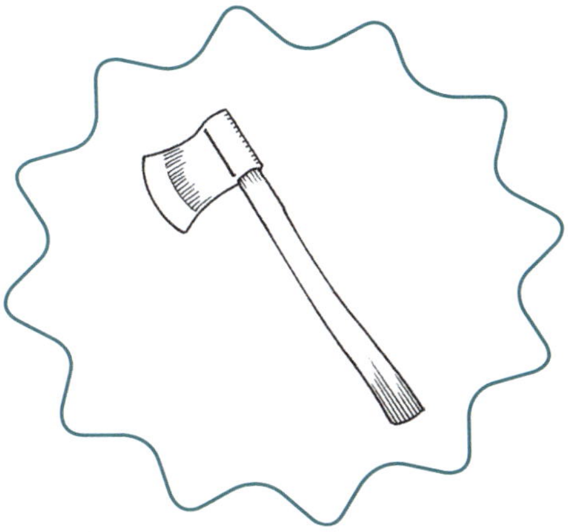

Handwriting

Track these letters

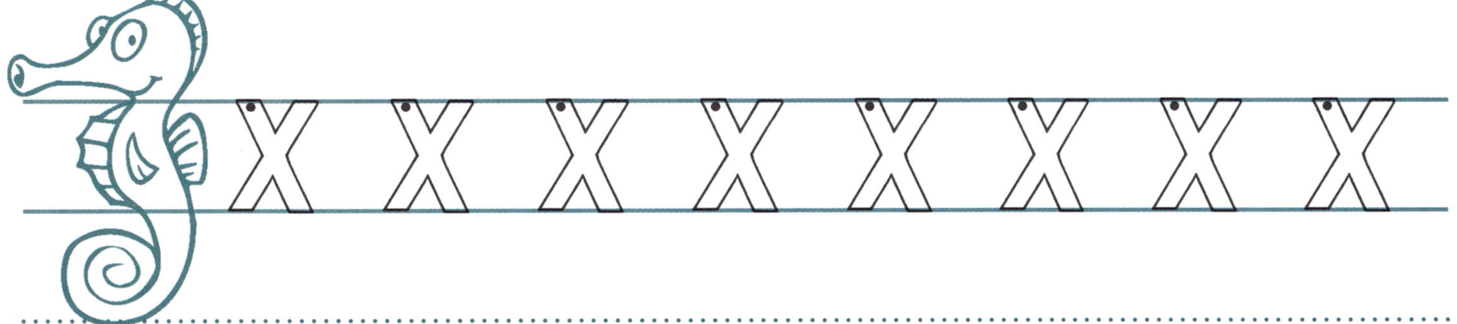

Trace these letters

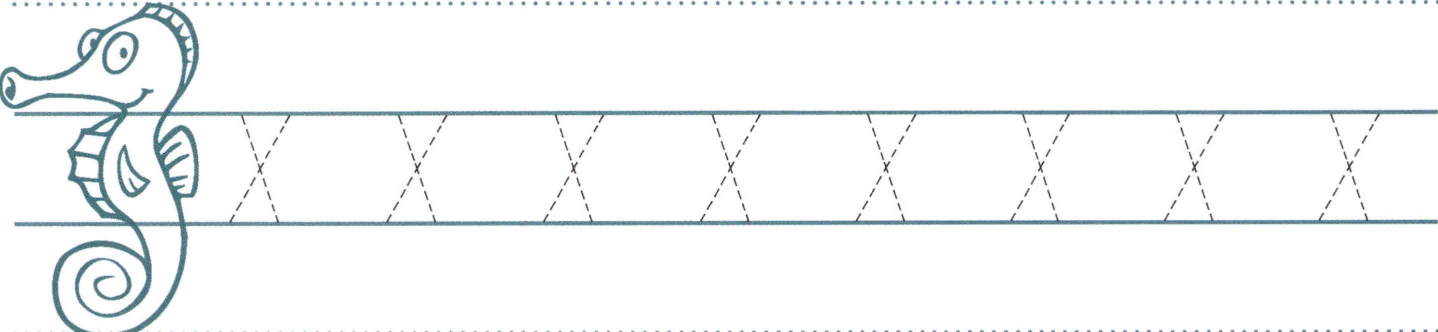

  ISBN: 9781925726343

⋆ Review ⋆

Say the names of the pictures below.
Circle the 'q' if it begins with that sound or the letter 'x' if it ends with the 'x' sound.

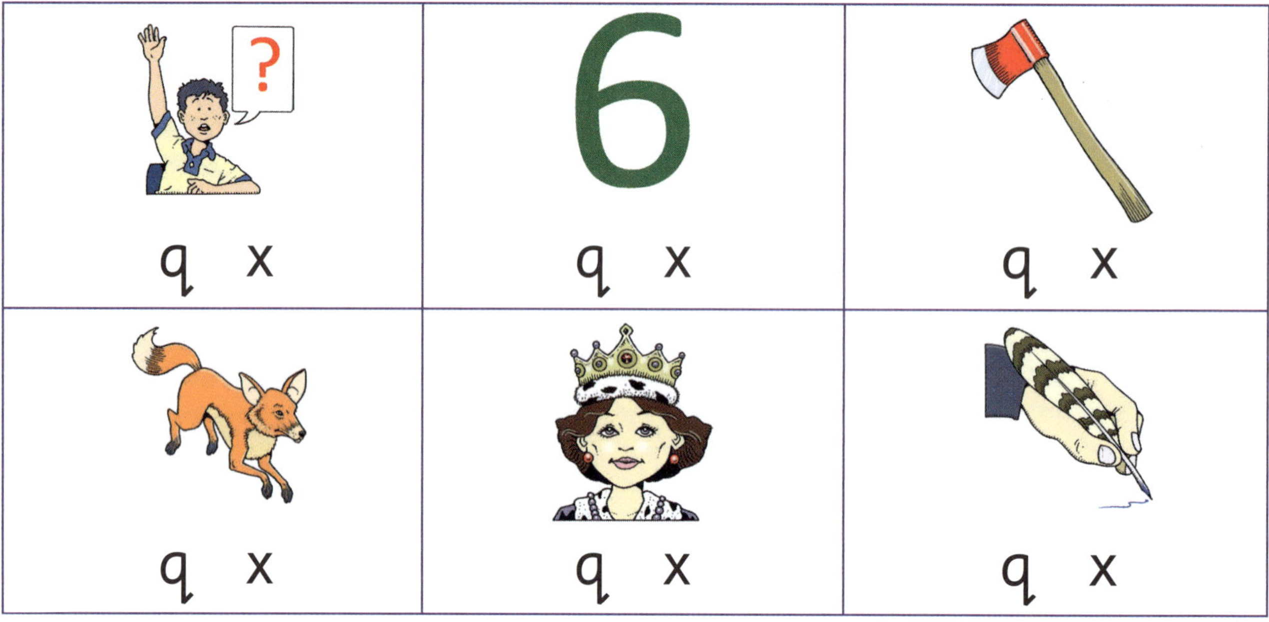

Say the names of the pictures below. Write the beginning sound of each word.

Say the names of the pictures below. Write the end sound of each word.

6		
________	________	________

Decoding

Now you know these letters and sounds:

s a t p i n d m g o c b h e u r f l j k v w y z q x

You can blend them to make and read these words.

Say the sounds	Blend the sounds	Read the word
Point to each letter as you say the sound.	Slide your finger from one sound to the next as you say the sound.	Point to the word as you read it.
qu i t	qu‿i‿t	quit
qu a ck	qu‿a‿ck	quack
qu i d	qu‿i‿d	quid
qu i z	qu‿i‿z	quiz
b o x	b‿o‿x	box
f o x	f‿o‿x	fox
m i x	m‿i‿x	mix
s i x	s‿i‿x	six

Read the words. Draw lines to match them to the pictures.

  ISBN: 9781925726343

Spelling

Now you can read these words, you can write them too.

Trace the words. Then write them on the lines below.

quip quiz quack

quick quest quoll

six box mix

fox fix wax

Choose letters you know to complete these words.
Read the words.

qu__ll __ix qui__

f__x qu__ck __ax

  ISBN: 9781925726343

Spelling

Say the names of the pictures below.
Stretch out the word to hear the sound at the beginning, middle and end. Write the words on the lines below.

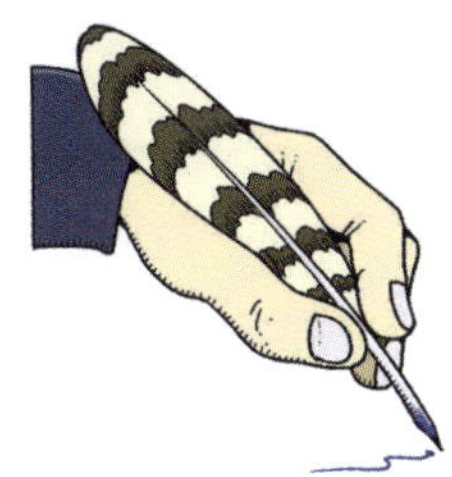

6

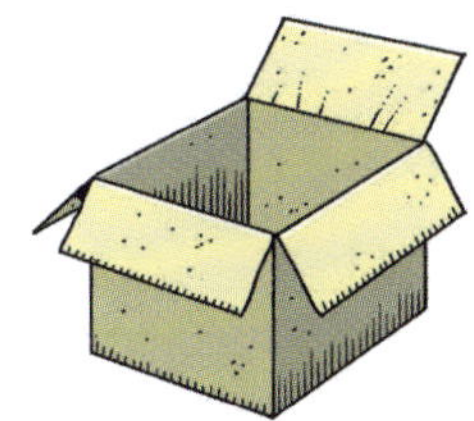

  ISBN: 9781925726343

High frequency words – Set 6

Learn these words.

was	mother	father	they	into
good	Mother	Father	They	away

Comprehension

Read the sentences. Draw a picture to match.

We had a quiz. I was good. I was quick.	Mother and Father got into a car. They went up the hill. They went down the hill. They went home.

The big red fox has a box. The box is big. A duck is in the box. The duck said, "Quack!"	"Where is my quoll?" said the boy. "My pet quoll is not here. It ran away." The quoll went into the tent.

  ISBN: 9781925726343

Comprehension

Look at the pictures. Read the sentences. Write in the missing word.

The quoll is in a big red ___ ___ ___.

Mother duck has six little ___ ___ ___ ___.

The quick ___ ___ ___ will jump the log.

This sentence is jumbled. Write it correctly on the lines below.

ducks Six little hill. went up the

  ISBN: 9781925726343

⋆ Assessment ⋆

Decoding

Read the words. Draw lines to match them to the pictures.

hill

tent

quoll

bin

zip

frog

dog

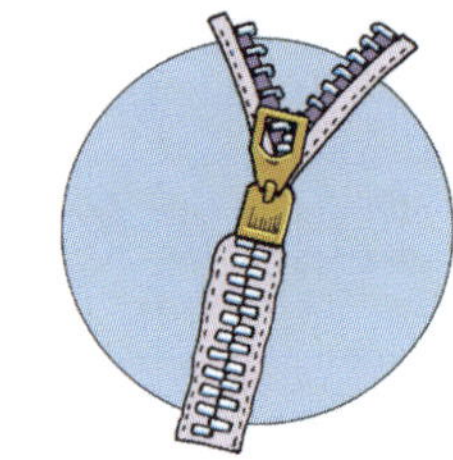

fox

cap

jam

yak

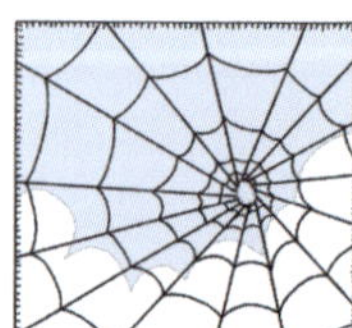

bus

vet

web

  ISBN: 9781925726343

Spelling

Say the names of the pictures below.
Stretch out the word to hear the sound at the beginning, middle and end. Write the words on the lines below.

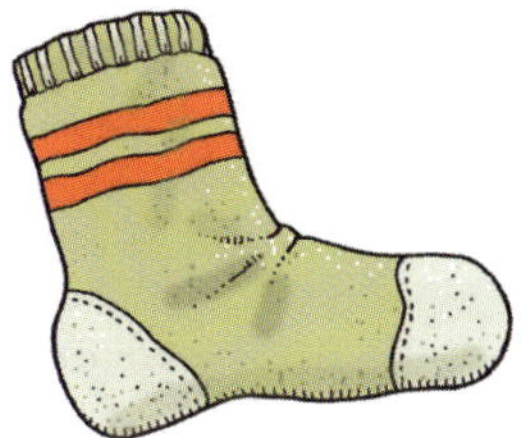

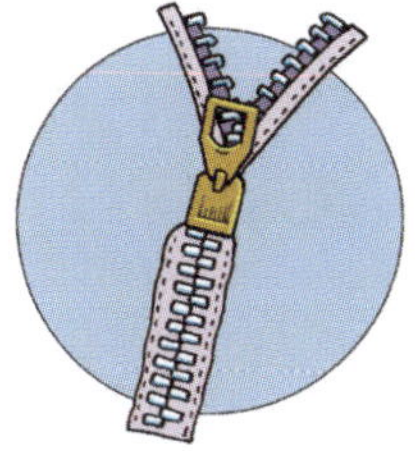

  ISBN: 9781925726343

Consonant sounds

Use letters you know to write words that rhyme with the pictured words.

hat ___at ___at ___at ___at ___at

pan ___an ___an ___an ___an ___an

bug ___ug ___ug ___ug ___ug ___ug

hen ___en ___en ___en ___en ___en

sip ___ip ___ip ___ip ___ip ___ip

dot ___ot ___ot ___ot ___ot ___ot

Comprehension

Read the sentences. Draw a picture to match.

I have a top. My top is red. My top can spin.	I like to run in the sun. It is fun but I get hot and I have to stop.

The girl has a pet pig. It is a big pig. It can dig in the mud. Will you dig in the mud too?	The red hen has some eggs in the nest. I like that little egg best. It is for me.

  ISBN: 9781925726343

Comprehension

Read the sentences. Write in the missing word.

The man has a big
___ ___ ___ cap.

The big pig is in the
___ ___ ___ ___ ___.

Mother is on the
___ ___ ___.
She has some eggs in her back pack.

This sentence is jumbled. Write it correctly on the line below.

eggs. and Mum to said ham the get

  ISBN: 9781925726343

⋆Decodable words⋆

Note: Plurals with final 's' are not included in the word lists.

UNIT 1 DECODABLE WORDS (S, A, T, P)

at	sat	pat	Pat	asp
app	sap	tap	spat	

UNITS 1 AND 2 DECODABLE WORDS (S, A, T, P, N, I, D, M)

mat	Nat	map	nap	add
mad	pad	sad	am	dam
Sam	an	pan	Dan	man
and	sand	ant	pant	stand
stamp	snap	span	tan	damp
spam	mass	tan	Stan	Pam
in	din	sin	tin	pin
mint	tint	dint	stint	spin
it	sit	its	pit	nit
spit	mitt	dim	Tim	dip
sip	tip	pip	mist	did

  ISBN: 9781925726343

UNITS 1, 2 AND 3 DECODABLE WORDS (S, A, T, P, N, I, D, M, G, O, C, B)

cat	cap	gap	bat	act
camp	bad	can	ban	band
bin	bit	cot	pot	tot
dot	not	got	cop	top
mop	bop	on	don	con
bond	odd	sod	pod	nod
mod	god	cod	Tom	dog
togs	cog	bog	sob	dob
mob	gob	cob	bob	big
pig	dig	bib	cab	tab
gab	nab	scab	nib	snib
bag	sag	tag	stag	nag
gag	bind	cost	stop	

  ISBN: 9781925726343

UNITS 1, 2, 3 AND 4 DECODABLE WORDS (S, A, T, P, N, I, D, M, G, O, C, B, H, E, R, U)

rap	hat	rat	had	hit
ham	ram	hand	ran	him
rim	hip	rip	has	hag
rag	hot	rot	hop	rod
hog	hob	rob	hid	rid
rig	rib	us	bus	nut
mutt	gut	cut	but	hut
rut	up	sup	pup	cup
pun	nun	gun	bun	run
mud	cud	bud	sum	mum
gum	hum	rum	dug	mug

UNITS 1, 2, 3 AND 4 DECODABLE WORDS
(S, A, T, P, N, I, D, M, G, O, C, B, H, E, R, U)

bug	hug	rug	sub	tub
pub	dub	cub	bub	hub
rub	pest	test	nest	mess
best	rest	set	pet	net
met	get	bet	ten	pen
den	men	Ben	end	bend
mend	bent	tent	pent	rent
rant	hen	Ted	tend	Ned
bed	red	hem	egg	peg
Meg	beg	must	dust	rust
grub	pram	sun		

  ISBN: 9781925726343

UNITS 1, 2, 3, 4 AND 5 DECODABLE WORDS
(S, A, T, P, N, I, D, M, G, O, C, B, H, E, R, U, F, L, J, K)

fab	fad	fan	fat	fed
fell	fill	fib	fig	fin
fit	fist	fog	fun	fuss
flap	flop	flan	flat	flit
from	frog	frock	lab	lad
lag	land	lap	lass	led
leg	lend	let	log	lock
lop	loss	lot	luck	pluck
lack	black	block	brick	jab
jack	jag	jam	Jan	jet
jest	job	jog	jot	jug

UNITS 1, 2, 3, 4 AND 5 DECODABLE WORDS
(S, A, T, P, N, I, D, M, G, O, C, B, H, E, R, U, F, L, J, K)

just	Ken	kit	kip	kiss
kin	skin	kid	kick	if
cliff	sift	rift	off	soft
cuff	buff	huff	muff	puff
stiff	stuff	back	hack	pack
rack	sack	tack	stack	deck
fleck	heck	neck	peck	buck
duck	muck	suck	ruck	tuck
stuck	truck	lamp	bank	sank
tank	clank	crank	Frank	drank
prank	plonk	bill	kill	dill

UNITS 1, 2, 3, 4 AND 5 DECODABLE WORDS
(S, A, T, P, N, I, D, M, G, O, C, B, H, E, R, U, F, L, J, K)

hill	gill	mill	nil	pill
sill	till	still	pal	bell
dell	fell	hell	sell	tell
doll	poll	toll	dull	cull
gull	hull	mull	lick	flick
Dick	Mick	pick	Rick	sick
tick	lid	lip	limp	dock
cock	mock	sock	tock	ill
help	left	rocks		

  ISBN: 9781925726343

UNITS 1 TO 6 DECODABLE WORDS
(S, A, T, P, N, I, D, M, G, O, C, B, H, E, R, U, F, L, J, K, V, W, Y, Z)

vat	vet	van	vent	wet
wit	win	wed	wag	wig
wick	web	well	will	yes
yet	yep	yap	yip	yen
yon	yam	yum	yak	yuck
yell	zit	zip	zap	Zen
zed	zag	zig	buzz	fuzz

quest	quit	quip	quin	quid
quack	quick	quell	quill	quoll
quiz	sax	six	tax	next
nix	dux	max	mix	cox
box	rex	fax	fix	fox
vex	wax			

  ISBN: 9781925726343

⋆ High frequency words ⋆

Unit					
UNIT 2	I UNIT 2	a UNIT 2	the UNIT 2	this UNIT 2	is UNIT 2
	see UNIT 2	A UNIT 2	The UNIT 2	This UNIT 2	on UNIT 2
UNIT 3	here UNIT 3	look UNIT 3	that UNIT 3	he UNIT 3	my UNIT 3
	Here UNIT 3	Look UNIT 3	That UNIT 3	He UNIT 3	My UNIT 3
UNIT 4	has UNIT 4	have UNIT 4	to UNIT 4	said UNIT 4	like UNIT 4
UNIT 5	you UNIT 5	me UNIT 5	are UNIT 5	go UNIT 5	down UNIT 5
	You UNIT 5	too UNIT 5	with UNIT 5	little UNIT 5	come UNIT 5
UNIT 6	we UNIT 6	no UNIT 6	where UNIT 6	some UNIT 6	going UNIT 6
	We UNIT 6	No UNIT 6	Where UNIT 6	boy UNIT 6	girl UNIT 6
UNIT 7	was UNIT 7	mother UNIT 7	father UNIT 7	they UNIT 7	into UNIT 7
	good UNIT 7	Mother UNIT 7	Father UNIT 7	They UNIT 7	away UNIT 7

ANSWERS

Review and Assessment Sections

Please note that answers may vary slightly for some questions.

UNIT 1

Page 16	Beginning sounds	p, t, s, s, a, a or p p, t, t, a, s, p
	End sounds	t, s, p
Page 17	Spelling	sat, pat, tap, pats, hat, app

UNIT 2

Page 26	Beginning sounds	m, d, n, n, i, m m, d, d, i, n, i
	End sounds	m, n, d
Page 28	Spelling	sip, mat, tip, pin, map, din

UNIT 3

Page 38	Beginning sounds	g, c, c, b, c, g
	End sounds	g, b, o, c, o, b
Page 40	Spelling	cap, bag, big, dog, cog, cot, cat, dog, pig, bat, top, bin
Page 43	Comprehension	dog, bin, cat The dog can see the bat.

UNIT 4

Page 52	Beginning sounds	r, e, h, h, u, e r, h, e, u, r, h
Page 54	Spelling	hut, leg, lip, rug, cup, rest, hen, peg, nut, ten, mug, sun
Page 57	Comprehension	tent, ran, nest The bug sat on the big red rug.

UNIT 5

Page 66	Beginning sounds	f, j, l, k, f, j l, k, f, k, l, j

	End sounds	l, k, f
Page 68	Spelling	lap, duck, jam, doll, lit, lock bell, leg, lock, jam, doll, truck
Page 71	Comprehension	truck, big, black, hill I have a red sock and a black sock

UNIT 6

Page 80	Beginning sounds	z, y, y, w, v, w z, v, w, y, z, v, v, y, w
Page 82	Spelling	vet, win, zip, well, yak, zap vet, web, yak, van, zip, buzz
Page 85	Comprehension	boy, mud, web The yak went down the hill.

UNIT 7

Page 90	Beginning sounds	q, x, x, x, q, q q, q, q
	End sounds	x, x, x
Page 92	Spelling	quoll, mix, quill, fox, quick, wax quack, quill, quick, six, fox, box
Page 95	Comprehension	box, eggs, fox Six little ducks went up the hill.

ASSESSMENT

Page 97	Spelling	well, sock, truck, zip, duck, six
Page 98		**hat** – mat, sat, pat, fat, cat, hat, rat, vat **pan** – man, fan, pan, can, nan, ran, tan, van **bug** – mug, jug, lug, dug, fug, pug, rug, tug **hen** – men, pen, den, fen, ken, ten **sip** – dip, kip, nip, lip, rip, tip, bip, pip, yip, zip **dot** – cot, hot, not, lot, tot, got, rot
Page 100	Comprehension	red, truck, bus, Mum said to get the ham and eggs.

  ISBN: 9781925726343